# DIGITAL OR DEATH

DOMINIC MAZZONE

ISBN Paperback: 978-0-9939573-0-7
ISBN Hardcover: 978-0-9939573-2-1
ISBN E Book:    978-0-9939573-1-4

# DEDICATION

This book is dedicated to everyone that ever took
the time to wonder and the leap to succeed.

# CONTENTS

# PREFACE

The Preface of a book is like getting hassled at the airport after landing at your vacation destination. All you want to do is get on it with it, but first you have to go through the baggage claim mosh pit, car rental upsell, immigration interrogation, etc., before you finally get to enjoy your vacation. So, instead of this being like a cranky immigration officer, let's talk about Rocky!

Yep, Rocky the entire series -- the movies that completely screwed up an entire generation of kids who are now adults. How did it screw us up? Well, for instance, I thought that there was no way that anyone could beat me in a fight no matter how big they were because the little underdog could always win. That definitely got me into a few scrapes in my 70's white sateen Italian Stallion Jacket. And every summer I told myself that I was going to somehow transform into a bigger, better, stronger me — cue the montage music because it was all possible if I worked really, really hard. All I needed was the right sweat bands and the will to try. In fact, my buddy Steve and I ate two dinners every night one summer and worked out before and after just to live the Rocky "non-stop" work ethic. It made me think that I could always get up after being knocked down.

Wait a second. Maybe Rocky wasn't as bad as I thought. That last delusion was probably a good lesson, and wanting to transform into a bigger, better, stronger me wasn't a bad lesson either. Whooaa ... working really hard to achieve that transformation was also a positive lesson. Oh my God, has a Rocky Complex been directing my personal

iii

and business transformations for my entire life? As embarrassing as that sounds, I think it has!

Was there something like the Rocky Complex in your life inspiring you to change?

Transformation is one of those strange things in life that *can* actually be forced. In fact, that's how it happens most of the time because the catalyst for change usually is an act of will. If you look at all of the Rocky films, Rocky's will is what makes the pre-transformation or transformation happen.

Everyone has transformed themselves at one point or another. Whether you had the Rocky Complex or not, we all share some experience of transforming ourselves — whether we wanted to or not! You would think with all of this personal experience, business people would consider a digital transformation pretty easy. But, they don't and it's the reason it usually sits in limbo for the majority of businesses.

The big issue is this — because we all own computers now, we think we understand digital. However, Digital Strategy, Digital Transformation and ongoing Digital Evolution are some of the most misunderstood areas of business today. To be blunt, we are all "digital stupid" to some degree or another and that is nothing to be embarrassed about. I am supposed to be a digital guru and people always come up to me and ask if I have heard of this company or that app, and often I say, "No." It's the truth because technology moves so fast it's beyond our capacity to upload all of it to our brain. There is just too much to find, try, install, and use, over and over again.

This book is to help you start thinking Digital Transformation and once you get there to encourage you to break out some of the Rocky Complex and take the first step. Every time I speak publicly my motto is, I don't want to talk to you — I want to change how you look at the world, at business, and at your business, and tune your mind to think digital.

This book better do that, and if it doesn't I want you to go to my website dominicmazzone.com and tell me. If this book does transform your thinking go to dominicmazzone.com and tell me how it worked! I would like to know if this book helps or fails you. Either way, let me know your story because when you digitally transform a business — interesting things happen!

One more thing. I use Amazon as an example in this book a lot. I don't love Amazon, I don't hold any Amazon stock, I don't have a side deal with Amazon for this book or anything else. In fact, I am not even going to predict if they are going to be profitable or insolvent in the future. I just think they are one of the living breathing examples of Digital Transformation and a company that is constantly on the edge of it. So don't hate on me or Amazon for giving them their due.

Lots of acknowledgement to important people in my life is at the end of this book. You'll meet some of these people throughout and it might make you actually read the list.

Yo Adrian, start the book!

# 1
# DIGITAL REALITY HITS HOME

Picture this. It's Friday night, I'm married, it's snowing, my son is 3 years old and I'm taking him on his first trip to Blockbuster to pick out a movie. This is a big deal for him — and me because for years I've been looking forward to having a son who's old enough to go on a Blockbuster trip so we can snuggle up and watch a movie. Sure, it's going to be Winnie the Pooh, but I'm game.

We get there. The little guy runs around, grabs movies off the shelves and I very gently put back the copy of Scarface he wants. We go to get ol' Pooh Bear, and lo and behold, somebody has rented it. In fact, all of the Winnie the Pooh movies are rented, and Tigger too. *SOB*.

We find something else and, yes, it was all worth it, because the little guy was happy. Of course, when I return the movie, it's late because he wanted to watch it 15 times and, of course, I was subjected to the famous Blockbuster late fees.

Fast forward two years later. At this point, the little guy knows exactly what he wants because he is Batman crazy and tonight we are going to watch Batman. We do our Friday night trip to Blockbuster and guess what? You got it, no Batman. The little guy doesn't understand what's going on, gets upset, and so does his little sister, because she always has his back. I'm trying to find something they can watch and a 5-minute trip turns into a debate as complex as the debt ceiling fight between Republicans and Democrats. Now, we're all miserable, and why? Because that was the world we lived in before the prehistoric movie rental business (now called the content delivery business) was digitally transformed. That was only 2009 and look how far we have come.

Digital Transformation sounds like a complicated concept but the pillars that it stands on are not. I've digitally transformed an entire industry and that means you, at the very least, can digitally transform your business, too. Now, the question you and everyone else faces is, "How do I digitally evolve this old beast of a business I have?"

To answer that you first need to understand why so many new start-ups are killing so many old businesses. It's simple. New start-ups don't have any baggage and their digital business models are like phoenixes being born from the ashes of countless businesses without the vision or courage to change. The businesses that don't transform their stale traditional business models are being annihilated by dynamic models that embrace the incredible opportunity to smash the "same old, same old" and forget about what business is — and concentrate more on what it can be.

So, if you are reading this and feeling fat-cat happy because you have a solid business that has been around for a while, let me shake you vigorously out of your fantasy.

The days of starting a business and leaving it alone to pump out money for the next 30 years are over. If you're not a business owner and feel comfortable in your job, let me remind you that the days of being an employee for 30 years with a nice fat pension at the end are over. That's over and it's not coming back.

Why? Constant competition and evolution. Constant evolution of technology and evolution of business models by competition both new and old...constantly! And the trick to surviving is: don't survive — win. Because it is not a trick, it's a mindset—a mindset that keeps your business model constantly digitally evolving.

Did you notice how many times I said constantly in the last paragraph? That isn't bad editing, it is to remind you that your mindset has to be relentless.

OK, everyone suffers from ADHD brought on by overstimulation in our society. And to keep this simple for you while your phone is ringing, beeping and vibrating I have boiled down all of my knowledge for Digital Transformation into four easy points. I call these the four pillars of Digital Transformation:

1. Wonder Theory
2. Revolution Delivery
3. Dynamic Interaction
4. Digital Hooks

You might be wondering what these are. You are going to know them intimately after reading this book, giving you a great foundation to digitally evolve. If you don't, read it again, so you don't crash and burn and let a competitor rise out of your ashes.

# 2
## DIGITAL DIE-OFF

We have heard about the frogs, fishes and bees that are experiencing massive die-offs and … we are about to see it in business as well. We are about to witness the dying off of legions of businesses that are either too lazy, too dumb, too scared or too slow to transform themselves. Sure, this has always happened before, but digital evolution will exaggerate the effects.

We are about to witness what is going to be one of the more interesting time periods in business, because it is going to be a combination of baby-boomer businesses going into succession and the next generation making a big decision. That decision will be to remain in denial and keep the business running as it has for the last 30 years, or wake up and accept the need to digitally transform to keep up. I have seen both scenarios and the ones that try and go with the status quo will look like guys trying to sell CD players at an iPhone Convention.

Digital die-off is going to be a reality and will be a tremendous opportunity for those that embrace transformation and a death sentence for those that don't. But you don't need to listen to me; use your eyes and ears. Think about what has happened in the past 10 years. Ask bookstore owners about Amazon. Ask Blockbuster about Netflix, and for that matter, ask the cable companies about Netflix. What about record stores? Ahh… iTunes and countless other online sources of music …how many record stores are actually in business anymore? My apologies to all you vinyl junkies out there because I love the sound too, however, what rules in these situations? Digital or death.

Oh, and it's not just industries that were easy to digitize. How much business have companies like Peapod, Netgrocer and Fresh Direct taken away from grocery stores? Yep, clunky grocery stores with all those atoms and molecules to move around have been digitally transformed — because people don't go into them anymore. Everyone thought people might buy books online but they'll never forgo the experience of going to the grocery store. Wrong! Old people like going to the grocery store, and even I like going to the grocery store on occasion because it's a novel experience. My wife, on the other hand, doesn't want to go to the grocery store for the 100th time this month. And if we feel this way, how the heck do you think a 20-something that has grown up on digital feels about it? They prefer texting to live conversations and WOW, they even break up by texting.

The ones that digitally transformed actually transformed industries. They not only transformed themselves to compete, but they were the trailblazers that laid down the track for others to digitally transform. The ones that didn't have already met their deaths, or are on life support. Digital or death.

Back in the day — I mean only eight to ten years ago — the big buzz word was business transformation. Now, you can't even talk about business transformation without considering Digital Transformation. Can you think of any business models that can compete on a meaningful scale that don't have a serious digital component?

OK, someone reading this might think their business is a B2B business that has its customers locked up and a Digital Transformation is not that important. One word for you, denial! From manufacturers to importers, to tailors, to golf coaches, to plumbers, digital isn't just important, it's a matter of survival. I guess if you were an illegal arms dealer that might be an exception. Another exception might be the government but even they aren't safe from digital ignorance. Obama proved that during his first election by using a digital strategy to raise campaign funds. It worked brilliantly. He also demonstrated if your whole legacy is based on a healthcare program that is based on a website that doesn't work, all that digital brilliance is quickly forgotten.

Digital Transformation is everything and everywhere and has

become a living, breathing, sometimes fickle thing you must pay attention to at all times.

Let me state this again. If you have not put together a plan to digitally transform your business, or at least put together a digital strategy under your current model, the death of your business is imminent. It may not happen tomorrow and might not even happen for years, but it will end up becoming a statistic of the digital die-off.

I WANT TO CHANGE YOUR MINDSET. I want you to look at the entire world as a digital opportunity for your business, other businesses, and even your day-to-day life so you are not a part of the digital die-off. I want to show you how to start thinking about Digital Transformation, recognize the opportunities, plan for it, and even how to start its execution. We are going to shake up your brain and talk about real and creative examples and I promise to give you as many tools to help you as I can. Also, everyone that has bought this book will get to log into one of my courses for free to help you further your evolution.

By now you have to be asking, who is Dominic Mazzone and why does he think he is qualified to show you how to digitally transform your business? OK, here comes my credibility pitch.

I am a serial entrepreneur. I started my first business when I was 16 and by the time I was 19 I had done everything from starting a car detailing business, to multi-level marketing, to starting a strawberry business, to promoting bands in Tijuana, Mexico (yes, you read that correctly). I have worked for large corporations, conducted business with C-level executives in Fortune 500 companies, and was responsible for managing hundreds of millions of dollars of business.

I've owned a web-hosting company. I started a commercial real estate investment fund (great idea in 2006, not such a great idea in 2008). I co-founded the first internet funeral company and digitally transformed one of the oldest and most un-transformable industries on earth (while successfully pissing off just about every player in the industry). The customers were really happy and the industry angst meant I did it right.

I'm the founder and managing partner of a consulting company called Smashbox Consulting Inc. that focuses on Digital Transformation. I work with multiple companies creating and executing Digital Transformation strategies. I am constantly creating new businesses, providing management consulting, helping incubate companies, and sitting on advisory boards of several companies.

If that is not enough for you to feel comfortable, at least keep reading based on the fact that I have been vetted by the press. NBC said, "It's a cliché to say that someone has seen it all, but well, Dominic Mazzone has certainly seen a lot" and the Canadian Business Journal has called me "Canada's Digital Guru." I have been featured by both American and Canadian media in newspapers, television and radio, including Bloomberg, Fox, NBC, CBC, The Globe and Mail, Toronto Star, Chicago Tribune, NPR, Profit Magazine, Realtor Magazine, and a bunch more ... and some of those were really fun -- and some were frightening.

All of that would mean nothing without the fact that I am a freaking hurricane of energy and I absolutely live and breathe this stuff, because I love it. I mean love it. The only thing I love more than transforming a business is my wife and kids and I am really crazy about them.

So if you are ready to take your mind to another level, let's continue.

# 3
# WHAT IS DIGITAL TRANSFORMATION?

## BLOCKBUSTER... A CAUTIONARY TALE

What is Digital Transformation? This is one of the most important decisions facing businesses across the world and it's unbelievable it's hardly discussed and when it is discussed, people don't get it. Accenture came out with a statement in October 2013 that CIO's (Chief Information Officers) must embrace Digital Transformation. Well, I have a fair amount of respect for Accenture and I hate to take a headline and beat them up with it, but Digital Transformation is so much more than just I.T. alone. CEO's need to embrace it, CFO's need to embrace it, CHO's, CTO's, CMO's, all and every COO, directors, employees, everyone needs to embrace it. Sure the CIO's and CMO's are the ones the burden is going to fall on for execution, but vision needs to come from everywhere, and it sure as heck needs to come from the top. To try to help you better understand it I have put together my definition of Digital Transformation.

*Digital Transformation is the deliberate and ongoing digital evolution of a company, business model, idea, process, or methodology, both strategically and tactically.*

Note I use the word *ongoing*. There is no way you can embrace Digital Transformation without knowing the transformation is only as good as the technology — and the technology changes incredibly fast. What's great today will look like a rusty old Buick with the wood paneling tomorrow. (However, those seats facing the back window were brilliant — way to copy that Tesla.) What looks like a business that will run forever on a static model will look like a Blockbuster store two years from now.

Oh yes, Blockbuster. I mentioned them in the beginning of this book because they are the absolute poster child of not embracing Digital Transformation. Let's think about this for a moment. Blockbuster was out there opening stores, renting videos, charging late fees, employing legions of zit-faced teenagers and smashing any new competition like wayward bugs on the highway. The company changed hands a couple of times and while all of this was going on, they ignored the growing threat of a little company called Netflix.

Netflix started up in 1997 as a somewhat traditional mail-order model where you rented a DVD, they mailed it to your home, you dropped it in the mail when you were done and avoided the pain at the video store. Enter Digital Transformation. These guys are progressive enough and agile enough to figure out that the model, though effective, isn't sexy enough. By 1999 they change their entire model to a subscription-based model where you rent like crazy and don't worry about getting your knuckles rapped for late fees. By 2007 they had mailed out their billionth DVD.

Here is the question … after watching the music business get absolutely spanked by the internet, plus the advent of delivering digital content via the web, and with Netflix gaining ground, was anyone awake at Blockbuster? Did they have any idea they were off the cliff, like Wile E. Coyote, running on thin air?

Netflix, on the other hand, was well aware of what was coming down the pipe. Once again, they knew that their model, though effective, wasn't going to be sexy anymore, and they brought their streaming service live in 2010. Even though there were some growing pains, the company turned itself from a mail-order company into a streaming titan. Blockbuster should have been on the forefront of this because Blockbuster was the brand name when it came to video rental. They tried after the fact but it was definitely too little, too late. Netflix smashed them with a digital hammer by transforming their model first.

Some Digital Transformations are huge and monumental like Netflix, but others are not, and don't have to be, to realize the benefit.

Every industry has the ability to digitally transform in some way or another. The only question is when do you start, and how many times? I say how many times because an industry, and a company for that matter, should continually evolve and never feel like they reached the finish line. I think the biggest issue with many CEO's / business owners is the misconception that Digital Transformation is a project. It's not. It's a mentality, because digital is always changing and evolving and you need to change with it. If that's not hard enough, your team also needs to evolve.

That is a difficult task and sometimes your immediate team can be poisoned. Poisoned because there is a phrase that exists that shuts down many new ideas. That phrase is, "Well, that's how we've always done it and it works."

Just because something works doesn't mean it's the best way of doing something. While that phrase is shutting down the minds of lazy management, all I hear is OPPORTUNITY. So much opportunity that with a little technology evolution you can turn an old way of doing something and digitally transform the process and create new revenues and cut costs. This is exciting stuff when you're a part of it.

So let's get into it and look at some of the pre-steps to Digital Transformation. Admitting to yourself that there are issues within the business that needs to be addressed is sometimes the most painful thing to do, and it's your first step.

# 4

# PRE-STEP TO TRANSFORMATION

## WHAT SUCKS ABOUT YOUR BUSINESS?

When I was 13 we moved from Chicago to San Diego. Needless to say that is a rough age for a kid to move, and even though I had delusions of California grandeur, it was mighty tough. I can't begin to tell you how different Chicago was compared to San Diego back in the isolated 80's. It was like another planet with strange and hostile inhabitants with messy hair, sandy feet, and everyone was named Dude.

After I finished 8th grade in relative obscurity, I started my first band with three friends that summer. Overnight, I became one of the most popular kids and was no longer the outcast from Chicago. We played at birthday parties, high school parties, school functions, and anywhere they would let us play and the band started to become our identity. Soon, we were viciously defensive, and anytime someone mentioned any other band we cut them down as only 15-year-old punks could.

That lasted until, one day, I went to see another local band that had been signed to a record label (that was still a big thing in the 80's) and something incredible happened. I let down my guard, sat back and enjoyed the music. In fact, I enjoyed it so much I was whooping and yelling, clapping and whistling. The pendulum swung all the way back and I became a fan, and I had an epiphany. My band sucked. Not only were we awful, but I was an awful drummer. And right after a worse thought occurred: how many people listened to us and said, "Wow, he sucks, and so does the band"? That was the moment I began my practice of constant self-examination, including how I would judge my ventures moving forward.

There's a fraction of books to help you self-analyze your business and career when compared to the avalanche of books out there about self-analysis for the individual. I find it far easier to ask why something bothers me, than what bothers me about my business. I think when you have worked so hard to create something, accepting that all that hard work resulted in something less than your definition of success is the last thing anyone wants to think about, let alone admit. Sometimes, you need to gain perspective about your business and that either comes from you, or from someone outside of the business.

"Your business sucks" is a brutal message but when it's delivered and accepted something amazing happens – it is welcomed with a sense of relief. It's almost like classic psychology 101 for business — tear it apart, admit there is a problem and it feels like a weight has been lifted. Once we know there is a problem in the business we can fix it but the problem will stay there like an everlasting zit unless we consciously expose it and deal with it.

AN EMBARRASSING TRUTH ABOUT MYSELF.

People pay me handsomely to come into their business, bring all my fire and ideas, and fix what's wrong. I can look at businesses all day and see how to help make them successful, but when it comes to my business, I'm an idiot.

In a perfect world I'd hire myself to look at my business. My business is successful, but it wouldn't be as successful if I didn't do a lot of self-examination, and have someone help me ask, "Why does my business suck?" Fortunately, I practice what I preach, and I have an amazing mentor and I trade consulting with a genius friend with a perfect business mind. We just beat the hell out of each other's businesses

We all need an intervention when it comes to admitting what's wrong with our businesses. Denial is understandable — people feel like their business is an extension of themselves. How many times have you heard someone refer to a business as their baby, or their child, or their spouse? Like my first band, our business becomes our identity and with that comes a lot of ego, insecurity and defensiveness. Hence, very rarely will we break down our walls and perform serious self-examination. That's not surprising — if we self-examine we know it will lead to change, which threatens our identity. However, you have to do it. This has been written about over and over in all kinds of self-help books for the individual, but I don't see this practiced very often in business.

Again, the pre-step to transformation is to break down everything you hold dear in your business to root out everything that is wrong. In fact, every time I speak publicly, I record it. Afterwards, I watch myself, even though it is incredibly painful. But it's simple — if I want to improve I have to study my performance and identify everything that is wrong. Even though I am the expert I have to say, "Dom, why do you suck at speaking? Why should you never be allowed to speak in front of people again? Why should you not consult businesses on Digital Transformation and growth?" Then, I find the issues, fix them and go out and create success by being the Digital Guru and the most electric, entertaining, exciting speaker around— all because I challenge myself to be better.

When you finally stand on your desk, stomp your feet and shout, "Why does this business suck and deserve to die!" you will have made the first and biggest step to taking your business to the next stage of its evolution. Sometimes, you need help when it comes to finding out what's wrong with your business.

Here's an easy fix for that. Bring all of your key people, and especially the troublemakers, into a room with a whiteboard and start making a list.

- What are all the reasons customers don't buy from us today?
- Why should customers not buy from us ever?
- Would I buy from us?
- Why would a potential customer not buy from us?
- Why don't we have more customers?
- Why don't customers buy more things from us?
- Do we have anything more for them to buy?

- What do our customers hate about us?
- Why would a potential customer not trust us?
- What is the most clunky thing about our business?
- What is wrong with our customer service?
- What is wrong with our products?
- Do we deliver our products and services in a timely manner? Faster than our competition?

The list can go on and on and this can also be done with a business colleague. Most CEO's know other CEO's and these are some of the most qualified people to get help from. I've performed these sessions in all of my businesses and, inevitably, we discovered all the things about the business everyone already knew deep-down. But we were so busy being the champions of the business the thought of being critical ran counter to the culture. However, once we sketched out what was wrong it wasn't a huge insurmountable thing. It was just a list of points that needed to be addressed one by one.

In fact, at intermittent times I felt the name of our online funeral business, Basic Funerals, was an issue. That hurt because I was the one who came up with it. Sure, it was a great name for a niche, but we could have branded ourselves better, attracted a bigger niche, and been much more successful. However, the name was incredible for getting press, so in that sense it was amazing. If and when I do it again, lesson learned.

To close on this point, we don't know what is wrong with our business until we have the courage to ask ourselves *why.* When we give ourselves permission to perform a 3D investigation into what is wrong with our business, then we can begin to fix it. That is Self-Help for Businesses 101.

## WHAT "SUCK" SESSIONS TELL YOU ABOUT YOUR CULTURE

If you do what was suggested and bring in your management and trouble makers and ask them to tell you everything that is wrong with your business, and you see a room of faces with tight lips and a look of pain, they are either constipated or more likely you have a culture that is too scared to say anything. Start the session telling everyone all the things **you** think are wrong with the business — make sure they know you're serious — then, keep it loose and open.

In general, as the leader you need to encourage a culture of brutal openness and honesty in these sessions. Openness creates a safe environment for creativity that will help transform your business and lay the groundwork for its continued evolution. Make sure everyone understands that not only are they free to speak, but the ones that do, get the respect from you, the boss.

## HIT THE IMAGINARY NUKE BUTTON ON YOUR BUSINESS

If the idea of finding everything that is wrong with your business wasn't enough to spark a ton of new ideas and overall energy in the business, this next part will really get you going. In the evolution of every business you need to ask yourself a question that may seem counter-intuitive. How would I destroy my business, and my industry? To be precise, the question is: If I were a *competitor*, how would I destroy my business?

That's right, get a little bit of a hate-on about your business, and figure out how you would take it out like an assassin. Think about how you would do it with a sniper rifle (no money), and then how you would do it with a nuclear bomb (lots of money). Both ways are effective, but it makes sense that a lot of innovation comes out of no-money scenarios because, sometimes, money is the innovation-killer.

You may find this exercise one of the most exciting and frightening experiences of your business life. It will make you peel back all the parts of your business where you are weak because, remember, you are thinking like a competitor trying to smash your business and take your entire market. You are that annoying little start-up out to expose every weakness of yours, while bringing a fresh new concept to your customers. You are the person that is going to figure out how to blow up the Death Star.

What usually happens during this exercise is someone blurts out, "We can't do this, it will cannibalize our business." Here's what you do — tell them to pipe down, and if it was you, give yourself a hard crack across the face.

Stop worrying about cannibalizing your business, because your competitors are planning just that — or doing it. Stop thinking this is 1999 and business moves slow. You have to lead and continue to evolve that lead because competitors are going to be coming out of the woodwork in the next two to five years because it is just so easy to get a business going these days. In fact, in 24-48 hours I can have a full blown business up and running with a website, addresses, phone numbers in multiple regions, countries, and continents, and begin to digitally advertise. That is how fast a competitor can get into a position to start to chip away at your market share.

Now, imagine five, ten, one hundred, even one thousand new competitors doing that every day. That is the world we live in today. If you think you've been around for 20 years and your customers won't skip to competitors offering a better platform, better customer service, better tools, or a better price because of loyalty, you are dead wrong! Loyalty is a cage match and smarter, better, stronger always wins by knockout or slow submission.

Let me back that up with a little data. Nielsen did a global survey of loyalty sentiment in Q1 of 2013. They did this on a separate basis around the world but the global numbers are important. Nielsen asked businesses which attribute would encourage them to switch brands, service providers, or retailers. Folks, the numbers don't look good for the loyalty advocates out there:

- 41% would leave for price
- 26% better quality
- 15% better service agreement
- 10% better selection
- 8% better features

Do you know what this all means? If a company came and offered better pricing, better quality, a better service agreement, better selection, and better features you could lose a substantial amount of your customers. In the real world that is not dictated by surveys you wouldn't lose 100% but even the biggest doubter has to admit this little piece of data says losing a portion or a majority is very possible. So instead of giving them a reason to leave, give them a reason to stay, and give potential customers a reason to switch. Find out what sucks, ask yourself, how do I blow up this business, and turn that cannibalistic fear into opportunistic revenue!

I am in good company with this line of thinking. The CEO of Panera bread, Ron Shaich, when asked about his upcoming digital transformation of Panera in a Time Magazine article by Josh Sanburn from April 2014, he said the whole idea centered around a main idea, "How would he compete with Panera if he weren't working for Panera?" That is a guy who gets it.

Do it now! If at this point you are still saying it would be impossible to transform your business, I want to show you that just about any business is a candidate. I am going to make it extra hard on myself and use an example of an industry that seems like it would be almost impossible to Digitally Transform.

# 5

# ANYTHING CAN BE DIGITIZED

## THE DIGITAL CARPETING BUSINESS

The carpeting business is as ancient as the dusty bazaars of Baghdad with hagglers that would make a used car salesman shake, so you may think there is not much room to digitally transform this tired old business. All right — let's say I was brought in to help out Jimmy's Carpets. Jimmy's has the best carpeting around, but his biggest issue is he can't differentiate himself from the rest of his competitors. As well, he has huge expenses coordinating delivery and installation after a sale. He loses precious dollars and time sending out a crew with all of their knives and irons to an appointment that is a no-show.

When I hear this kind of story I get excited, because I know there are amazing things that can be done to make this business better. What we need to do is eliminate the issues and come up with a differentiator to drive revenue. What I call the Digital Hook. (More on Digital Hooks coming up in Chapter 7.)

First thing I am going to recommend is create a carpet preview app that allows Jimmy's customers to take a picture of rooms in their home, upload the pictures, and then they can add in the carpeting he carries right into those pictures. This would allow people to see the carpeting they want in their actual room — and Jimmy's Carpets now has a powerful sales tool.

Now, customers are drawn to Jimmy's site because they can see what their room is going to look like with his carpeting (and no one else's). This inhibits Jimmy's customers from going to someone else to purchase carpeting because who knows what the competitor's carpeting will look like in their house because Jimmy's competitors *don't offer* a carpet preview app.

Plus, there's a bonus — what's great about my patented carpet preview app is it has the potential to become a valuable tool for a customer base that I didn't have access to before. What do I mean? Think of it — designers constantly face what they think will look good and what they think their clients will like. What if they could show their clients what something looks like in their house before they buy it? Now, designers are selling for me using my app. This goes for my sales people too, because now they have a better tool to sell carpeting inside my stores. I have an incredible web-based app that gives me a serious edge over my competition. You can see why I refer to this as a Digital Hook.

It doesn't stop there. When you go down the road of Digital Transformation, sometimes it's a highway and sometimes it's a scenic route that allows you to discover all types of new things. What about the issue of confirming appointments? This is a massive time waster for a lot of businesses and the carpet business has the same problem. So how do we fix this?

According to our definition of Digital Transformation, we use the technology that is available. Let's start with the order process. Pretty well everyone can give you a cell phone number. I know, I know, some people don't have a cell number, but at this point 91% of people have a cell phone according to a 2013 PEW Research study, so let's deal with the majority.

OK, Jimmy's Carpets' client's order comes to the warehouse. It's entered into the system, which then looks for an open calendar entry. A predefined algorithm says 1,500 sq. ft. of carpeting for 4 rooms is going to need 3 guys for a 3 hour appointment, and we need an extra 45 minutes because there are eight stairs. The system finds an open time, and shoots out a text message asking the user for confirmation of the time and date we are suggesting. Once a confirmation is received, the system also sends out a reminder text the day before to ensure the customer is going to be home.

I just cut Jimmy's expenses by removing the need for someone to book all the appointments, and someone else to confirm the reservations. That is a lot of calling that doesn't need to happen anymore and that is big savings. I also cut down on my no-show clients, which saves Jimmy money because he's not sending out a van full of guys with carpeting, knives, and irons. Plus, now, instead of sitting around and costing Jimmy money, they're busy. Sure there are going to be some people that can't agree with the date and time provided but I am digitally transforming for the masses and we can deal with that in "Phase 2".

It also hits the supply chain because there will be more people coming to Jimmy's site through his app which is going to sell a lot more carpeting, thereby giving Jimmy more buying power and leverage with his suppliers, thereby increasing his margins. Some of you doubters out there might be complaining that this app is going to cost tons of money and there is no way a carpeting company can do this. Doubt and fear — more poisoning. This is 2014, apps are cheap and some of the stuff I am talking about will be off the shelf software plug-ins.

Have I ever worked in the carpeting business? No. Do I know anyone in the carpeting business? No. Am I some kind of genius? No. I swear I wrote this sitting in my kitchen as I thought about it — because my head is tuned to business and the business part of my brain is tuned to digital. I did, however, use this example recently at a conference I spoke at, and we had a ton of fun with it.

The point here is — if you tune your mind to think digital you'll find Digital Transformation everywhere. The opportunities are all around us and sometimes they aren't completely obvious. Sometimes what looks impossible to transform is just waiting for us to create an amazing Digital Transformation out of nothing.

### DIGITIZING SOMETHING OUT OF NOTHING

When I was 19 and going to USC I spent a lot of time going to nightclubs. Yeah, I had a fake ID and that would get me in the door. But it was a buddy of mine that got us in. He was a crazy SOB and unbeknownst to me dealing in not-quite-legal substances. I never quite understood why the red velvet ropes at nightclubs parted like he was Moses, mostly because I was such a straight arrow.

What a life, though. We would show up to the lines of people outside all of the clubs like the infamous Roxbury or Bar One in

L.A. and we would walk right through the door. There was even a club called Poo Nah Nah that was set up like a Maharajah's tent with pillows everywhere and people just laying around or dancing. Leave it to the sober guy to be so naive that I didn't realize they were all on drugs. Mickey Rourke would come cruising in on his motorcycle and even freakin' Doogie Howser was allowed in and he couldn't have been more than 16 at the time. It was a crazy experience that left me with lots of vivid memories.

The one thing I remember clearly is everyone, and I mean everyone, wore Levi's. From Mickey Rourke to the guy working as a dishwasher, everyone had on Levi's. There was enough of a mania around Levi's that people would fill their suitcases with Levi's, go to Europe and sell them to pay for their trip. Everyone was Levi's crazy.

So how is it kids from the past 20 years have no idea what Levi's are and really don't care? If you don't believe me, ask one of them. Levi's are no longer cool. That made me indulge in a little Wonder Theory (more on that soon). How could you make Levi's cool again by digitally transforming pants? You could add lights on them but you are going to look like a five-year-old, or like you belong at a rave back in the 90's. My insight occurred when my dear friend Andreas provided me the answer by sending me a YouTube link with the message, "Drumpants, wish we had this when we were playing music."

Well, the same generation that doesn't know about Levi's came up with a campaign on Kickstarter to digitally transform pants. They are called Drumpants. With this product, you actually turn a pair of pants into a full-blown drum set including a speaker and headphones. You can plug Drumpants into your computer and record with them. OK, maybe you don't drum on your pants but there are lots of people who do and they would love to sound like a full-blown drum set. However, the founders of Drumpants understand that Drumpants are only the beginning and they also need to transform. I spoke to Lei Yu, co-founder of Drumpants. She and her partner have a vision that all kinds of devices like video games, slide show presentations, etc. can all be controlled from the wearable tech they invented. She also stated, "Drumpants is so much more than drumming. It is unique wearable tech."

Great idea and forward looking. My point is — if you were Levi's could you use something like this to get that demographic excited about what you're doing or, at the very least, interested? I bet this technology would vault Levi's back to the outer edges of the cool-o-sphere or at the very least get people talking about Levi's again.

This is a great example of a Digital Transformation waiting to happen. If you want to transform, you must think beyond your preconceptions or even what you might view as physical limitations. In this case, you need to think about what people do with their pants, instead of the actual pants themselves. It's sheer brilliance. Go to www.drumpants.com and check it out.

How about another product that seems impossible to digitally transform? There is actually a product called the True Tester love bra. This bra only unhooks if the woman's heart rate reaches a certain point, indicating she is in love ... although, lust might qualify as well. It's a Digital Transformation of the bra and, though it's a gimmick, the Japanese company that came up with it is getting a ton of press.

My point is if you think beyond your current business incarnation and allow yourself to evolve into what you truly can be, you'll not only make more money, but you'll probably start having more fun.

# 6

# WE CAN TRANSFORM ANYTHING

## ...AND HAVE A LITTLE BIT OF FUN

If you are still sitting there thinking that your business can't be transformed or that it isn't important, then you are going to get caught in the digital die-off. There are some very high profile Digital Transformations that have been recently announced. As mentioned, Ron Shaich, CEO of Panera Bread is initiating a Digital Transformation and, to put this into perspective and show how serious he is about this, he is spending $42 million on Panera's Digital Transformation of the food industry. The Digitally Transformed Panera breads are going to let you walk into a store, order up what you want on an iPad, and swipe your credit card. Then you walk up and get your food. The take-out system is supposed to be just as seamless. As exciting is that is, and as hard as it is to imagine the food industry being transformed, let's look at a few industries that really need it.

### GOVERNMENT

Here's a place that doesn't have the money to support itself, has a bloated workforce that defies logic, has service levels that decline the more employees it has, and continues to operate as if it were the 1970's. The majority of governments around the world need a Digital Transformation, in most cases from the federal level all the way down to the state/provincial and municipal levels.

How is it private companies derive tons of benefit from technology but it's Kryptonite for governments? Whether it's registering your

23

car, filing taxes or communicating with anyone, governments don't embrace digital and when they try to, they do it poorly. To be fair, there are exceptions to this rule but for the most part the only thing you can do online everywhere is pay parking tickets.

How many times have you spoken to a government worker from the IRS or CRA and they tell you they don't have email? Are you kidding? My nine-year-old has email but the federal government who wants 50% of my income doesn't? Security is usually the reason given for this but if the CIA and the White House can use email, get hacked, and continue to use it, can't we give the folks at the IRS email? Bad policies put these workers at a disadvantage and scream inefficiencies. How many times have you been told you have to send a ton of documents via snail mail — or to their fax machine that doesn't work, so please send everything again, and again, and again?

Think how much time, energy and paper is wasted. Our governments are train wrecks when it comes to technology, and the opportunities for the use of technology are limitless. The lack of debate about the use of technology to make things more efficient in government is almost criminal. The only choices they give themselves is to either cut costs or spend more money but have you heard any discussion about spending money on technology to cut significant costs? When talking about the government we don't need a revolution, they need to embrace Revolution Delivery (more on that coming up. See how I am warming you up?).

### AIRLINES

If there was ever an industry that was the boulevard of broken dreams, it has to be the airline industry. I'm not going to pretend to understand the airline business. Even the experts have a hard time making money in that crapshoot. But I do see evidence the airline industry is ripe for Digital Transformation.

Some of you may sit there and think it's not possible to digitally transform an airline. There are too many atoms and molecules. Wrong. That model is as old and rusty as a rotting TWA DC-10 on an abandoned runway. Remember TWA? It was one of the big four and went through not one, not two, but three bankruptcies before being acquired by American Airlines. Talk about needing a transformation.

Here's my point: airlines suffer from all kinds of problems, but from a revenue standpoint airlines suffer from empty seats. The reason they suffer is because they can never tell how many people are going to be on the plane until it's about to take off. Sure, everyone books ahead, but people cancel flights all the time. The airline charges a change fee, but they still have planes taking off with empty seats. At this point you might be asking, "Why don't they just throw a seat sale a day before the flight, or even 6-12 hours before to ensure that the seats are full?" Because the industry is afraid that if they do, everyone will wait until the last day and buy last-minute for a lower price and cut into their margins.

In reality, there are tons of people that book at least a few days ahead, like business people and other people that book much farther ahead, like families taking a trip, and old people. (We all know that grandmother or grandfather who loves to book six months ahead of time and pack two weeks prior.) But even with all this advance booking there are still empty seats.

Let's open up our digital brains — what if an airline created an app called Smash Seat? Imagine that 6-24 hours before one of their planes took off, Smash Seat shot out to tens of thousands of app holders 2-4 seats for destinations of their choice. The price is discounted and whoever smashes the yes button on the app first gets the seat. If nobody responds after the first 30 minutes the price goes down further.

Of course, people would submit their credit card as part of the sign up for the app with all the disclaimers, blah, blah, blah, sales are final, to make this an instant process. Airline execs at this moment are shaking their heads calling me crazy, but how crazy am I? Smash Seat solves a big issue and provides a huge side benefit as well. Empty seats are filled, which is the basic issue, thereby generating more revenue for the airlines. The huge side benefit is this will turn into an absolute marketing and branding juggernaut.

The airline that does this will pop up on people's phones constantly keeping their brand in front of their customers. Whenever they think of flying they will think of the airline with Smash Seat first. Is the app holder going to be annoyed by all the flight deals? No way — we've given them choice (first rule of dynamic interaction). If they really want to go to a particular dream destination this app may be their chance, or maybe all they want is to dream about going. However, when they do need to visit their in-laws or somewhere else the first name in their heads is going to be Smash Seat, or the airline that put out Smash Seat. Take that to its logical conclusion — the first airline that does this can leverage this into brokering for all the airlines and take a little piece of their action.

We're rolling, but do you know what really makes this app a success? Gamification.

I know — it sounds like what made the Hulk green, but what gamification does is generate a whole lot of green. Gamification means you create a game from your business model or as a marketing tactic. Gaming is everywhere now and it takes a lot of different forms. The obvious form is Xbox, Nintendo and PlayStation. We are talking about a sizeable gaming population from 5-year-olds to people in their mid-40's. Gaming is the norm now because it has rewired our brains to crave it. It's as if we have to adjust all of our business models for the gaming psyche because that psyche is our society. So we should embrace it because gaming in one form or another and gamification is only going to get bigger and more prevalent.

If people want a game, give them a game. Smash Seat feels like a game because you want to win. Why do you think people get hooked on eBay? Because an auction is about beating the other guy and that is -- you guessed it, a game. You get so wrapped up in the competition that all of a sudden you have a garage full of stuff you don't really need, but it felt so good getting it — because you thought you were winning it.

Gamification is also spreading into digital advertising like crazy. Advertisers realized a while ago that people don't pay attention to advertising anymore. It's human nature to adapt and we've adapted to ignore advertising. Advertising on TV is struggling, and when I say struggling, I mean emergency room struggling. The model has its challenges. You pay big money to make a commercial. Then, you pay big money to an agency to book the commercial. Pay huge money to run the commercial — and what happens when the commercial runs? Everyone fast forwards through the ad on TiVo and that's if they are even watching TV on the TV. A growing number of people watch their favorite shows on anything but an actual TV.

Oh, and don't forget the people watching live TV are most likely out of the room, grabbing food or another beer, taking a bio-break, or looking at stuff on their phone while your very expensive commercial runs. Not to mention all kinds of new technology that skips you through commercials automatically. Look, I'll admit some TV advertising can be very effective, but humans have adapted and even when they are seeing a TV commercial they might not actually be watching it.

Don't think the web is completely insulated from all of this. More and more people are starting to tune out web advertising, and banner advertising especially. However, unlike TV, the web can be more creative. Advertising that moves, advertising that blacks the screen out, advertising that takes over your screen, YouTube advertising that you have to watch, the list goes on and on and changes month after month.

However, just seeing a commercial is really only half the story. The other half is that you want a viewer to be engaged or, at the very least, pay attention. Gamification helps to solve this in advertising by getting the audience to dynamically interact with your brand because you have someone entrenched in a game with your branding all over it. If you can get someone to play that game for even one minute while you are delivering your message or your brand, then you have just accomplished what TV advertising has not been able to do for the last 20 years—get people engaged.

Gaming has also become a bit of an addiction. An addiction that is powerful and not just from a social aspect, but also from a real physiological aspect. The guys at Tech Crunch pulled a study published from Nature's Translational Psychiatry back in 2011 that said, "*An international research team has shown a correlation between frequent gaming and greater volume of grey matter in part of the brain linked to an internal reward system associate with addiction.*" In other words, frequent gaming is changing our brains, and when you think about it, frequent gaming is becoming the norm. Harvard Medical School was on to this almost ten years ago when they published an article called The Addicted Brain which said, "*Researchers have already found resemblances between the brain scan images of compulsive gamblers and drug addicts. The idea of addiction to television, video games, overeating, or sexual behavior*

27

*may be more than a metaphor. Exploring the biology of addiction could lead to a deeper understanding of the sources of all human motivation and habit formation."*

My brain has been altered. Gaming has such a powerful effect on the mind that I remember actual scenes in games that I played 15 years ago and I probably played a fraction of today's norm. Can you imagine the next generation coming?

The real life example of this concept is the incredible success of the ALS Ice Bucket Challenge. This was one of the most brilliant marketing moves in the last 10 years. Think about it. A challenge is a game. Nominating other people to take the challenge gets other people into a game. Making it fun makes it feel like a game. Put all this together and you have a social phenomenon.

Gamification can come in all kinds of different formats. I think Domino's is really progressive in their thinking when it comes to their Digital Transformation with the launch of Pizza Mogul. It basically lets the average person become a "Pizza Mogul" on Domino's infrastructure. The average person signs up to their app, creates and names a pizza of their own, promotes it anyway they want with social media being the most likely choice, and then starts earning a piece of the profits. What better way to get people engaged in your brand and to use their free time promoting it! Brilliant and when you think about it, pretty simple as a digital model. Crowdsourcing in this way is just an offshoot of gamification.

Gamification in your model is an absolute key consideration whether it is in your marketing, or within your business model itself. Get your head around gaming and if you have a team, take them offsite, play a few games, and bring them together in a full gamification session where you challenge them to make your model, a portion of your model, the advertising, whatever … into a game.

# 7

# THE FOUR PILLARS OF DIGITAL TRANSFORMATION

There are definitely times in your life when an unconventional Ready, Fire, Aim attitude is what gets you launched and even successful. Many times, it will make you feel like you're being dragged behind a Harley ridden by a sadistic Hell's Angel across Nebraska.

Case in point: When I was 19 I seriously electrocuted myself trying to change the alternator belt in my car while my friend Sam laughed uncontrollably at what must have looked like a cartoon. Today, I know I should have unhooked the battery, but I wasn't mechanically inclined and I didn't have instructions. As a result, there is nothing that makes me more crazy than buying something without instructions, or at least a picture of what it's supposed to look like after it's assembled.

Consequently, I am going to give an instructional overview of The Four Pillars of Digital Transformation so you get the full picture. Speaking of pictures, you can see this in visual format in Figure 1-1 and notice that all of these are equally important. Each and every one of these four pillars needs a healthy dose of creativity (and guts). However, anytime I have digitally transformed businesses, these four pillars were critical to the overall success of the Digital Transformation. To truly embrace these pillars and tune your head to digital you have to let go of everything, especially doubt and fear. You need to get what I like to call "wonder" back in your life, and doubt and fear are wonder killers.

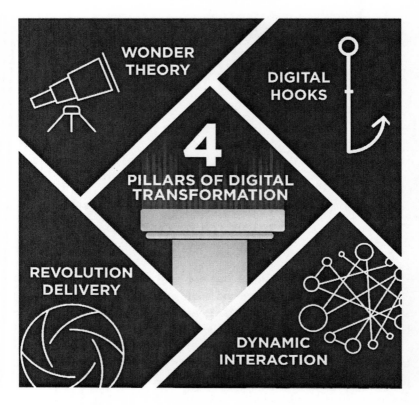

*FIGURE 1 – THE FOUR PILLARS OF DIGITAL TRANSFORMATION*

## PILLAR #1 - WONDER THEORY

Think back to the first time you rode a bike -- "I wonder if I can do it?" You never knew until you tried, but you were open to it. The first time you jumped off the high dive -- "I wonder what it will be like?" or "I wonder if I'll drown?" You didn't drown, but you would have never tried it unless you faced the fear because you wondered about the outcome. The first time you went on a date -- "I wonder what will happen?" You had to throw on a little of your dad's cologne and go for it. My theory is that most of the real rewards in life are on the other side of wonder. It is the one thing that will keep you innovative, current, and as a bonus, keep you young. I call this Wonder Theory.

Wonder Theory is when we allow ourselves the benefit, time and privilege of wondering through a problem, situation or opportunity while acknowledging the fear that comes with it, but not letting it stop us. Wonder Theory is the beginning of something incredible, if we allow ourselves to find out what is on the other side. We have to grind against the grain and push ourselves to allow the sense of wonder to come back in because when wonder comes back, we open the door to creativity and innovation. Give that wonder a chance, do a little bit of investigation and a new world of opportunities is going to open up for you. Ask things like, I wonder how to make this better, I wonder what our customers really want, I wonder what products we can sell, I wonder what customers we can sell to that we currently are not, I wonder how I can be a better leader, I wonder if our business sucks — and if so, how do we fix it?

Why have we stopped wondering? The overall speed at which we have to operate a business in the digital age only allows us to grind, not to think, and especially not to wonder. Admit it: you are probably grinding 95% of the time and only thinking about getting to the next task. The problem is day-to-day business constantly gets in the way of wonder. Think about it. While you concentrate on the business, and get stuck grinding it out, does that create an environment conducive to innovation or transformation? What can you do about it? It's this simple—shut it down at least 30 minutes a day to get perspective. Either choose something you really want to wonder about or do a little free-wondering.

When I was young, my dear friend Rob Valerio, who is a brilliant business consultant out of Los Angeles, introduced me to the now-popular phrase, "You need to make sure you are working on the business instead of just in the business."

What does that mean? Think about it — working in the business gets you stuck not only in the grind but also in the rut of doing things the same way without asking the question, "I wonder if there is a better way to do this?" There is not enough time while juggling daily tasks of running a business to ask this question. Business leaders never give themselves this crucial time to wonder, but great leaders do. Wonder Theory is working *on* the business.

But let's change that behavior, because tuning your mind is going to take a little discipline and a little bit of fun. Fun, you say? Absolutely, who the heck wants to grind it out? Digital Transformation is going to be a blast.

### DIGITAL EXERCISE THROUGH A LITTLE WONDER THEORY

This is a group exercise that I do with companies. It can be used for all types of different things with a little tweaking. When it comes to getting everyone excited and living the Wonder Theory, these are the steps I use:

1.  Grab three members of your senior team and walk out the door together making it an even number. Yep, walk right out the door because this doesn't work as well when you are sitting inside the office.

2.  Collect all cell phones. Laptops and tablets are OK but no email or texting. You need to focus.

3.  Identify one thing that is broken in your business that hampers you from generating more customers, or more revenue from customers, or something that is an expense you wish would go away, or identify a new direction for the business.

4.  Everybody gets 15 minutes by themselves to wonder-up a solution to the problem. You have to come up with an idea that doesn't just throw money or more labor at it. Technology usually can accomplish this so that's why you need your computer for research.

5.  Now, split into 2 teams and you get 30 minutes together to come up with the best mutual solution.

6.  Finally, all come together and in 20 minutes come up with the best mutual solution. (The time crunch helps with the focus.)

7.  Take that idea — vet it, plan it, budget it, and execute.

8.  Now here is the kicker – do this every 2-4 weeks. Yes, every 2-4 weeks.

I can already hear the complaining. "This is too much time taken away from the business, this will be too much change at once," blah blah blah. Well, don't do this and continue to grind it out. The only wondering you'll be doing is why your business has no life and innovation. You might find that this is one of the best and most fun things that you have done with your business in a long time and if you want to do more than just keep up, you need to do this — or something like it.

This is not to say that these are all going to be monumental projects. It can be as simple as changing how you qualify your customers by directing them to an online submission form or as detailed as outsourcing an entire department or digitizing portions of the supply chain. Don't let the scope of something that hasn't happened spook you. It's the process that is going to start tuning you and your senior management to Wonder theory and eventual Digital Transformation and once this happens, it is like a fusion reactor that just keeps creating energy. Too many ideas is a high-class problem. High-class problems are good problems so don't be a wonder killer. Great leaders wonder!

## PILLAR #2 - REVOLUTION DELIVERY

The word revolution has a lot of different definitions but a combination of them is what revolution delivery is all about.

One definition is, "a sudden, complete, or marked change in something," and "an overthrow or repudiation and the thorough replacement of an established government by the people governed."

Replace the government part with the tired old business models we are talking about. Customers that don't have choices will revolt and jump ship if someone is able to give it to them in a better way. In short, Revolution Delivery: deliver what the customer wants, how they want it, and be totally flexible about how you give it to them, and you will cause a revolution that persuades them to leave their current provider. This may not sound profound but think back to before there was an internet.

Let's go back to the 80's for a moment. Slip on your white suit jacket and roll up the sleeves like Sonny Crocket from Miami Vice. Let's pretend we're buying a car—not the fake Ferrari Daytona or the white Ferrari Testarossa that Sonny drove. I remember buying cars in the 80's as a 16-year-old punk and the only choices back then were to buy a new car from a dealer, or buy a used car from a dealer or a private party. If you wanted to find a used car from a private party, your only choices were to look in the classifieds in local newspapers, or back in California we had a publication that came out once a week that had cars listed. I could have sworn it was called Auto Trader but, supposedly, that was founded in the 90's. Anyway, those were your only choices. To find out who had cars for sale you had to go out and buy a bunch of different publications like the mainstream newspapers, local newspapers, plus the Auto Trader publication. Not to mention that if you lived in San Diego you were limited to the cars in San Diego County. You would have to repeat that process for Orange County, L.A. County, Riverside County, and so on, to increase your selection of cars. Does that sound like a pain?

As a result, I couldn't get what I wanted, where I wanted, and how I wanted it. If I wanted to buy a new car I was completely stuck with my local dealer and they could charge me whatever they wanted. The car industry, both new and used, forced me to work in their model, because I had no choice, and they knew they had a captive audience. Let's see how far this has come.

Currently, I live just outside of Toronto, Canada, and it is a well-known fact that within Canada we're screwed on pretty much everything we buy. Sure there are all kinds of excuses like the exchange rate and a smaller population than the US but in essence it is crap and we are getting gouged. The same products that come into the same port are sometimes priced almost half in the US what it costs in Canada. In addition, the Canadian dollar and the US dollar have been between 1-15 cents apart for the past 5 years. Because of that I chose to buy my car in the US and transport it. Here's what I did:

- Went on autotrader.com and searched the entire USA for a car

- I was able to find the exact car I wanted with very low mileage in New Jersey

- I was able to find it with the exact options I wanted

- Verified, via the web, that the warranty would still be honored when the car came across the border

- Verified, via the web, the total amount of tax and duties I would have to pay

- Contacted a local dealer with a Jersey accent like Tony Soprano, via the web, to check the car for me. The car was checked, cleared, and the report was emailed to me

- Now I knew I had a good car, I found a transporter and broker, via the web, and booked everything online

- There are all kinds of escrow services like escrow.com to handle the money/car exchange

- The car showed up at my front door 4 days later like a Christmas present with all the necessary paperwork ready and waiting for me to walk in and register it

DONE!

Number of cars for sale in Ontario that were the same model I wanted – 1.

Number of cars for sale in Ontario that were exactly what I wanted – 0.

The amount of money I saved from this process to get the exact car that I wanted – $15,000.

I got what I wanted (the car), how I wanted it (the right price), where I wanted it (delivered to my front door). There are people offering this service in Canada, but they wanted a $5,000 fee and acted like they were doing me a favor, so I did it myself. I created my own Revolution Delivery. Not only are the digital tools to do this out there and easily available, but I saved $15,000.

I repeated this process when we transformed the funeral industry. We gave people what they wanted (a funeral for a cheap price), how they wanted it (they could arrange everything on the web, we didn't package anything, we gave them exactly what they wanted, and didn't charge anything extra), and where they wanted it (we didn't own a funeral home so we didn't force people to use one). Instead, we provided funerals where our customers wanted them— golf courses, yacht clubs, churches, event centers, cemetery chapels — anywhere they wanted it.

That is Revolution Delivery. Netflix does it for movies, Google does it for search, Skype and Hangouts do it for calling and video conferencing. Android and iPhone do it for phones, and Amazon pretty much does it for everything. Your job as a business leader is to try and fit into your customers' model, not to force them into yours. The days of forcing people to do business the way you want are either dead or dying in every industry, because I promise you a competitor is right around the corner who is going to create Revolution Delivery for your customers and change the way you do business. Wouldn't it be better if you were the one starting the revolution?

## REVOLUTION DELIVERY— A FRICTIONLESS EXPERIENCE

Blackberry, oh Blackberry, you were my best friend. I will never forget my first Blackberry because you blew my mind. Wow. Email on my phone. Impossible. What followed was the phenomenal rise of Blackberry to heights that made it seem Biblical — and we looked upon them with awe. They brought Revolution Delivery to all of us. They gave us what we wanted (email), how we wanted it, and where we wanted it.

But under all that success was something that would percolate until it boiled over. Blackberry for all of its innovation was inflexible. Everyone did it Blackberry's way or the highway. Inflexibility was everywhere, from running an extremely proprietary platform that required equipment everywhere to support their famous security, to not opening the system to outside programmers to create third party applications for their users.

Being first to market and timing might have been a part of that. Then along came Apple with their touch screen. That took away all the friction of using a phone, and that rolling Blackberry ball suddenly seemed a little square. Blackberry's leaders thought, "Who cares about a touch screen?" but what they should have asked was, "Is it easier to use? Is there less friction? Can you do more with it? Do people like it? Do they like those apps?"

Do you remember trying to browse the web on a Blackberry before the iPhone? It was torture. The browsing experience on the iPhone was frictionless like a computer and light years ahead of Blackberry. What the iPhone proved was consumers will choose less friction over known comfort.

Blackberry thought their tactile keyboard would save them. It didn't, because as great as that keyboard was, it wasn't equal to the frictionless experience of the iPhone. Blackberry thought they still would have the business environment locked up, but they didn't make that frictionless either. They lost, and they lost more. Even after being crushed by Apple for years, and losing tons of market share, they still don't get it. When I first saw their latest phone, The Passport, I thought it was actually a joke from "The Onion." I would have called the phone square, but that actually describes it. It's an absolute horror. It looks like an attachment from an Atari gaming system from the 70's. Of course, it's touch screen, but it is still clunky compared to what's out there now with the exception of it being able to use Android apps. RIP Blackberry.

Is it possible that Apple will make the same mistakes Blackberry did and continues to make? Oh, I hear it now — howls from Apple's core market, or as I call them, The Apple Core. I know, for you, I have spoken Apple's name in vain, but try to keep your eyes open to what's going on out there — Macs, tablets, as well as the iPhone. I was a devout iPhone user but it started feeling like they were losing touch. Not to mention they kept putting out new phones that didn't really feel new at all. Even though the iPhone was a game-changing product and the Digital Transformation of the cellphone into the first smartphone, you have to admit it is starting to feel like the Apple way or the highway. Friction!

What if I don't like the iPhone screen size? What if I don't like how it feels in my hand? What if I don't like the accessories? What if there is functionality I don't like? TOO BAD!! It's the iPhone and you take what we give you. Friction. Whereas Android can be found on phones of all shapes, colors, sizes, even a waterproof phone.

Most people don't realize that, now, Android has 80% market share around the world. 80%! How did Android go from 0–80% in 5 years? It digitally transformed the marketplace by making the hardware the least important part. When all you concentrate on is the software (digital), you make that great and tell the world the phone isn't important — it's the user interface that matters. It's about making the experience better and better aka frictionless. In addition, you have all these multiple phone makers doing all the heavy lifting for you and, boom, you're more popular than iPhone in less than 2 years. That's right, Android came out in September of 2008 and the operating system surpassed iPhone by May of 2010. It became the world's leading smart phone platform by Q4 2010. That is astounding when you think about it.

I also disagree with predictions that Apple is going to surpass Android. I'm not saying it's impossible but I wouldn't bet on it, unless Apple digitally transforms itself and creates a frictionless way of offering their operating system to other phone makers. Google bought Motorola for a minute, which was outside their original model, but that didn't stop them offering the operating system to other phone makers. The Google model is the volume model and that will take some time to beat.

I moved, probably like many others, to an Android phone because of the flexibility and frictionless experience. Android is a product that gives all of the flexibility you want, and it feels like someone thought of you as the customer when they designed it.

This is Revolution Delivery. Give your customers the most flexible and frictionless experience possible. I mean totally frictionless. If there is something in your sales process that makes a customer hesitate, pause, or get indigestion, you should be overhauling it, now. If there is something in your product or service that you feel customers just have to put up with, change it. If there is a product or service you should be offering, offer it. If you don't have a sales and conversion process on your site, create one immediately. I mean right now so stop reading and take 30 minutes to wonder about how you can sell your service or product online. If you can't figure it out, find someone inside or outside of your company who can.

### FRICTIONLESS MEANS GIVING UP CONTROL

Do you remember waiting by the stereo with a tape loaded to go, waiting for that one song to come on so you could record it? Do you remember going to multiple stores looking for something specific you wanted? How about this: do you remember wondering about something, not finding anything in an already outdated encyclopedia, then going to the library and you couldn't find the answer there either?

We forget how little control we had then, and how much flexibility and control we have now. Sure, we were fine before but ... we had no control. Today is different. You want a song? Download it. You want something specific? You can find it online, compare prices and order it. You want to know your bank balance? It's right there online without you having to tear the house apart looking for that little book. You want the answer to something? Google! You want to buy almost anything you can think of? Amazon. Want to know what everyone else thinks about a product? CNET, Facebook, Twitter, Instagram, Pinterest, etc.

We take it for granted, but a good Digital Transformation gives flexibility and instant gratification to the customer and the customer loves it. If you think how we were once slaves to the analog world, you can appreciate how far we have come — and how far we have to go. There are plenty of industries and a ton of businesses that still haven't given the control to their customers. If only they knew and let go of the control, they would decrease their costs and generate tremendous amounts of revenue through the process.

In the world of Digital Transformation we flex to our customer's needs and learn how to fit in their model, not the other way around. Now, overall control resides with the customer. **Answer the question how can you give control to your customers, and you have taken a step towards discovering the catalyst to begin your Digital Transformation**.

Next step — how can you gain more customers by also giving them control?

Sometimes control can be as easy as putting prices on your site. I mention prices on sites a few times in this book because for 90% of the businesses out there it is the easiest and most important thing they can do. The company that puts prices on its site tells the world they are open and honest. They have nothing to hide, and the ground rules are set for a transparent and predictable relationship.

Pricing on your site makes the customer feel like they are in control. You have armed them with the one piece of information they really want to know. Sure, we are terribly impressed with your website and your client list and your testimonials, but how much is this going to cost! An additional benefit of putting pricing on your site is it tells the customer you are credible.

If you think about it, there are so many dead websites out there, sometimes it's hard to tell if you are dealing with a company that is still in business or one that put a site up 3 years ago and nobody is home. Pricing says you sell a tangible product, you are open for business and you can actually come up with the product or service if the customer pays. Nothing is more powerful than pricing on a site! If you don't have it, or you are sitting there thinking that it doesn't work for your industry, you should try harder to find some way to break with the norm, be a trailblazer, and make it part of your web strategy.

A small caveat is that some businesses are not conducive to advertising prices. Every business I have owned has shown pricing online. However, for Smashbox Consulting this is next to impossible as it is management consulting and every project is 100% different and I don't bill by the hour. Businesses that rely on heavy customization have difficulty showing pricing online unless the product or service is conducive to an online product builder that generates a quote. I am a big believer in these and if you can do it, make the investment.

Giving control through Digital Transformation needs to also include employees—jobs without some sort of control feels like jail. Employees are happiest when they feel there is some flexibility in their work life, and that flexibility feels like control. Always include and consider your employees—every one—in your Digital Transformation. There are all kinds of ways to do this but some of the most primitive are still not utilized by a lot of businesses. I was interviewed back in 2009 by Realtor Magazine about my belief that things like teleworking will rise massively. However, I am still shocked when I see companies unnecessarily paying overhead and chaining employees to their desks. Teleworking is obvious to create flexibility but there are so many other things that are obvious like friction in processes, bad supply chain communication, unnecessary data entry or taking a lot of information over the phone. These are the first places to give your employees control through digital. This gives them the tools to do their best job possible, and gives them control. They expect it when they browse and shop online. Work isn't any different. There is nothing worse than working in a broken system, and imagine their pleasant surprise when their work is easier, more effective, and free from mind-numbing tasks that can be digitized so they can concentrate on growing the business.

A transformation that solves employee issues inspires confidence and an overall feeling of satisfaction with their job. Personal control is the catalyst that will transform your business by transforming the workplace first. You'll be pleasantly surprised by how powerful your internal Digital Transformation can be.

GIVING CONTROL MEANS GIVING TIME

If you could sell time, you'd be at the top of Forbes 100 richest people in the world in a day.

Flexibility means time. It's the fundamental reason e-commerce works, and works so well. It's able to provide us with that one thing each of us wants so badly — time. E-commerce works so well that even bricks-and-mortar giants can't deny it. Costco's online division continues to grow and I think it will be, one day, one of the biggest parts of their business. When you think about it, is that really surprising? I may want what Costco has, but I sure as heck don't want to waste my time dragging myself through their warehouse and giant checkout lines. Take a look at any groundbreaking websites, business models, devices or applications that dominate the marketplace and you will discover many of them give you back a little bit of time. Usually, through Revolution Delivery.

Whether you went from a typewriter to Microsoft Word that allowed you to correct as you typed, or a smartphone that let you check your email without going back to the office, or Amazon that delivered the world to your door, or Facebook that let you feel important while socializing with multiple friends without all the effort, they're all different applications that save time.

Saving time is flexibility, and when you have the flexibility to do what you want, where you want, when you want *and* also get what you want when you want, you save time. Some people say time is the most precious commodity in the world — it's beyond that, because time is the most precious thing that exists. If you can give someone just a little bit of time, you are going to be successful.

Tear your model apart and find the time that is hidden there. Whether it's for your customers or your employees it doesn't matter. Time means flexibility and it is invaluable. If you can give your customers that, I guarantee you'll make a sale, each and every time.

***How do you know it's frictionless?*** A simple four-word phrase was hammered into my head by my mentor, Ed Minich. Ed is insightful and caring and that is probably why he is one of the shrewdest business people I've met. Ed has done a lot— he was a professor at McMaster University in Hamilton, Ontario, and he ran Otis in Canada for a long time and was incredibly successful at growing that business. He had tons of employees and had to deal with the regular barrage of information any CEO deals with. Except, Otis was gigantic and part of the goliath, United Technologies, so it was far more than most. Ed said whenever he would be updated by his VP's, Directors, senior managers, he would ask one simple four word question, "How do you know?" Initially, they would tell Ed, "Well, so and so told me." And Ed would ask again, "How do you know?" Usually after the second or third time they got it, and never showed up to a meeting without knowing.

If you have a sales and conversion process on your site, you should be examining it from head to toe. Does it make sense? Is it frictionless? *How do you know?* The best 87 dollars I ever spent was on third- party testing. There are all kinds of testing and functionality experts who will charge thousands — and some of them are worth it. In my experience, a site like www.usertesting.com blows me away. I would love to own this business because it makes a ton of sense. For $87 you get three complete strangers to go through your entire site for 10 minutes and record themselves. This is a mind-blowing experience because the things on your site that you think are interesting, may not be. The things that you think are frictionless are not. The things you think are not important, actually are. None of your staff can do this for you because they are too close and neither can your friends. Strangers are the key, and when you watch them go through the site, the experience is priceless.

When you interact with your customers digitally you must ask, "How do you know?" Never assume. Assuming creates friction. Find out the answer by using the data. We are in the world of Big Data and if you are not using it you are going to be smashed.

All of that Revolution Delivery needs Dynamic Interaction and to make that interaction smooth you need to be thinking about any and all of the friction within your business. Once that friction is gone, you are ready to engage through dynamic interaction.

## PILLAR #3 - DYNAMIC INTERACTION

Have you ever had a conversation with someone who continually talked at you? It's like listening to talk radio and you can't change the station. It's exhausting. It's the same with old-school advertising. All day long, your customers and clients are being talked at by advertisers and sales reps who want their money. The first question my mind asks the business that is advertising is: with all of this sales and advertising pressure you're putting on me, what are you going to do for me? What input are you going to give me for my output, and what output are you giving me for my input?

Keep that in mind and think about the Web. In the early days websites were pretty static. For example, if you went to BMW, or Ford or any of the big car companies, you would see pictures of cars and specs and that was about it. Can you imagine going to a car site today that won't let you build your own car? You input everything you want and they output your car. I love that, and so do millions of other people, because we get something tangible out of the experience.

Let's look at dynamic interaction from the beginning. Do you remember the first time you heard about a blog? I remember thinking, "What the hell is a blog and why am I interested in it?" It's too bad the term "blog" was coined because it is a really bad name for a great idea. If someone had said to me, "Hey, within minutes you can have your own personal magazine, newsletter, soapbox, whatever … and it is totally simple to get it up and running," I would have probably said, "Wow, that's amazing, where can I sign up?" Instead, I heard the word blog and thought someone threw up, so it took me a while to start my first one.

How did blogs become a major phenomenon and a must for businesses? Think about it. From a purely functional perspective, for the first time people could express themselves en masse on any subject, from thoughts on quantum physics and the existence of dark matter to how much you hate your boyfriend. You were in control and could publish and gain an audience for the low, low price of free! However, it was the foundation for so much more. It was also the first time a writer could get instant feedback via a comment because, before that, publishing was a one-way communication. The readers/ customers also experienced an output (comments back) for their input (their comments). Blogging was not only the beginning of social media — it was one of the first times that businesses had the opportunity to interact with their customers on the web in real time. That is Dynamic Interaction.

The dictionary definition of *dynamic* reads, "characterized by constant change, activity, or progress." I like the noun, too: "a force that stimulates change or progress within a system or process." When we engage our visitor so they feel like the experience was built for them and we provide them output for their input that is *Dynamic Interaction*.

At the start of any business you're not quite sure how your customers want to be engaged, but the first step is common sense. Let's go primitive and talk about your site. Do you think anyone wants to come to your website and take two minutes finding your phone number? Do you think someone wants to come to your site only to have to pick up the phone and call you for your pricing? Do you think potential customers are going to take more than five seconds figuring out what your business or site is all about? No, no, and no — because that is a whole lot of input for no output. Do you think your regular customers want to have to call you on the phone to order more product? No, too much repetitive input for the same output. Dynamic interaction is what retains customers once they have come in the virtual door. They want to be engaged either through great visuals, great tools, great content that educates them, or a great process that makes them want to hang out and come back for more.

This principle is valid off the web too. Customers don't want to call you and be transferred to 10 people before finding the right person. They feel the experience was not built for them. Customers don't want to waste time sitting on hold. They don't want to walk into your place of business and not be greeted by somebody. Zero or limited output for their input.

OK, we're starting to have too much fun. Time to talk about no fun at all: funerals.

When I transformed the funeral industry I knew that displaying a price online was going to be key. Believe it or not, it wasn't the industry norm, and trying to get a price out of a funeral director over the phone was like trying to get a politician to praise their opponent during an election. So, right from the start, not only did we provide pricing, but we let the customer build their funeral.

Depressing? Not for the people booking funerals because it was incredibly helpful. Did it give them output for their input? Absolutely. It saved time and money and put them in control.

If we go back to my carpet company example in the beginning of the book, you'll see that the app we created gave the customer an output for their input. They took a picture of their room and were able to pick and choose the best carpeting for them. It was easy and saved time — our carpet company delivered value in return for the visitor spending time on our site — output for input. Plus, because the app is useful to our visitor, it helps turn them into a loyal customer, and it engages them. Dynamic Interaction.

In each case, we can see that Dynamic Interaction rewarded the input and contributed to creating a Digital Transformation by anticipating the need(s) of our customer. There are so many ways that this Dynamic interaction applies. Let's look at another example.

I helped incubate a great company called Propel Active. Propel Active brings wellness providers like physiotherapists, chiropractors, and naturopaths to companies. When I say "brings them" I mean the doctors go to the businesses, set up in an office once or twice a week, and treat employees on-site.

Businesses love it because their employees don't leave work for appointments, and when the treatment is finished their employees are refreshed and ready to work. The employees love it because it makes their lives incredibly easy and they get the care they need, without all the hassle.

How does Propel Active use Dynamic Interaction within its model? It first started with Revolution Delivery. Propel thought about how the client would want to interact with them. Not the reverse. The first thing Propel asked, "What does our client want? What do clients not like about the current model?" Then Propel went further and asked, "If our clients want their therapy to feel like we anticipated their every need — what does that look like?" And they smashed the ideas of what was, and wasn't, possible. Instead of making clients come to Propel —Propel comes to their clients. This is not to say the clinic system doesn't have its place, but what brought me on board with Propel Active is that this idea is transforming an industry.

Propel Active built their business with Dynamic Interaction as a core principle.

Propel Active's clients can book online. Is it really necessary to speak to someone to do something as simple as book an appointment? The system works fantastically as clients see all the times available and choose what suits them. The system automatically sends a reminder to the client and even follows up with a feedback form to make sure their appointment went well. When the client schedules their appointment they can complete the forms they'll need for their appointment. It sounds like easy stuff, but it saves time and aggravation for the clients and the doctors. It makes them feel the experience was built just for them. Simple stuff.

There are other things Propel Active does to create Dynamic Interaction with its customers but those features alone are enough to make clients love Propel Active.

On the back-end, Dynamic Interaction is also in full effect. Here the vision is, reduce costs, make the system easy for clients, contractors and employees, and engage them the way *you* would want to be engaged. Once a patient has been treated, all of their insurance information is automatically submitted to the insurance company. Then the system automatically emails the patient a balance statement and link for a Visa/MasterCard payment. Here, the output is being given before the input.

Think about how much time that saves everyone — and how it helps Propel Active process payments quicker. All the doctors and therapists who provide services for Propel are part of a shared online calendar that shows them when they work, where they go to provide their services, as well as arranging for someone to cover them if they can't make an appointment.

This isn't rocket science folks, it's basic calendars in the cloud, and countless providers offer it. It allows everyone to see where they are booked, how they are booked, and updates in real time. That makes scheduling easy. It's all about ease of use and great output for input.

Dynamic Interaction is an absolute pillar of any Digital Transformation and the one that's most difficult to get right. But, Dynamic Interaction can be built in stages. You may get part of it at the beginning and build from there. In fact, once you start building it for your customers it becomes addictive. You keep trying to find new ways to interact and build value from any inputs they give you. After that, you will constantly try to come up with new ways to get those inputs and provide outputs that drive your business.

When it comes to digital marketing I always preach Dynamic. No matter how much traffic you send to a site or business, if a business doesn't successfully interact with their visitors once they arrive they might as well not be on the Web. Great Inputs + Great Outputs = Dynamic Interaction = More and More Revenue.

In closing, asking for the input is just as important as giving the output. Dynamic Interaction should be circular like a discussion. Can you imagine having a discussion with someone and they never ask you a single question? It's boring, it drains you and it's a waste of time. So stop your business from being a Chatty Cathy and bring a little Dynamic Interaction to the party.

## PILLAR #4 - DIGITAL HOOKS

As a professional musician (in what now seems like another life) I was introduced to the concept of "the hook." A hook is that special something in a song that somehow "hooks" you. It can be a lyric, or a melody, or a stupid nothing of a sound, but it is that little something you can't get out of your mind. Barry Gordy's Motown created one of the most successful music businesses in history by constantly creating simple unforgettable hooks and it has been the Holy Grail for everyone ever since. From the doo wop of "Baby Love" by the Supremes in the 60's, to the guitar riff from "My Sharona"(6 weeks at number 1) in the 70's, to the way Olivia Newton John sang "Physical" (10 weeks at number 1 to become the all-time Billboard chart topper of the 1980's) to the annoying "Macarena"(14 weeks at number 1) in the 90's to the totally insane *ringggrinnngggg* hook of the YouTube sensation of 2013 "What does the fox say?" (over 450 million views). What do all of these have in common? They all had hooks you couldn't forget and some of those hooks felt so natural you would never know they were there.

Business, and especially digital business, is no different. You need to hook people and keep them coming back — give them a special something that entices people to do business with you — preferably, through your model and dynamically through your site. The business or digital hooks I am talking about can be as varied as the musical ones I listed. When it comes to being social we think of Facebook—it gives the un-famous a little bit of fame. When it comes to note taking, Evernote—their hook is your note anywhere, anytime, on any device. Little known Only Coin saves pocket space by putting all of your credit cards in one piece of plastic and in fact, your phone can track it if you lose it (hopefully they get it launched out of Beta). When it comes to music we think of iTunes—they were one of the first to offer a broad range of music in a safe and easy to navigate digital marketplace. iTunes' hook was the ease and cool factor. Google Drive, iCloud, Amazon Cloud, Dropbox, give us freedom and peace of mind by freeing us from any device because our data is backed up in a virtual location. All of these things get us because their functionality is their hook.

The Digital Hook is one of the Digital Transformation Pillars and it can also be the culmination of all the other Pillars coming together. When you can really see or feel the hook, that is probably exactly what is happening. Sometimes, the explanation of the digital hook is in the name itself — I'm thinking of RingCentral, MailChimp, eBay, SalesForce.com, Evernote ... and the list goes on.

Everything I touch I try to give a hook. The funeral business had two hooks: the Digital Hook, an online quoting system that created an entire quote in front of the customer's eyes and allowed them to download it, and the Revolution Delivery/Choice Hook — customers got the funeral they wanted, where they wanted, at a low price.

Propel Active has two hooks: the Revolution Delivery Hook — going directly to the client, saving them precious time, and the Dynamic Interaction Hook — online booking and payment that puts choice and ease of use right at the client's fingertips through their desktop or mobile device.

Each of these businesses created hooks that work. Once you get your head tuned to this digital frequency, you'll see the successful hooks in business models, or the Grim Reaper looming over business models that don't have them. It's the first thing I try to find or create with the companies I help. I never rest until I find the hook.

I also never stop looking for new hooks, because once you find one you are going to want to find more. The evolution is inevitable.

You're going to start asking yourself, what has never been done? What can you really do that is massively different? What hook do your customers want? Keep asking again and again, because if that first hook is working, more may be waiting. If your business doesn't have one — get one, because your first hook is waiting for you to find it.

These next fundamentals are not necessarily pillars but they are definitely integral to Digital Transformation.

## COST

Anytime I contemplate digitally transforming a business model my goal is to generate more customers and revenue. In that process I try to reduce the overall price to the customer, reduce the overall costs, or both. What I'm trying to say is you don't build something whiz bang just because it's cool or because you feel like you need to do something new. You do it because the overall benefits are going to create more customers and revenue, and/or better margins and EBIDTA.

To be clear, I am not telling you to digitally transform your business to become a low price leader because I have been there, done that, and it is a lot of fun in the beginning but a ten-ton anchor around your neck as time passes. I am talking about solid financial gains to support the rationale for Digital Transformation.

Let me give you an example of what I am talking about. When I came up with the name Basic Funerals, it was probably the best and worst name we could ever have chosen. When I thought about the simplicity of the model, Basic Funerals just popped into my head. The name was the hook and I liked it because it told a market niche they could finally get a basic funeral for a price they could afford. However, the name overshadowed the real Digital Transformation and we were viewed as cheap even though the service was anything but, it was fantastic. The model itself reduced costs but I believe the name didn't tell the real story. That was our problem.

First, the funerals weren't cheap quality, they just cost less money but in my opinion we had ignored the majority of our market — people who wanted an affordable funeral but didn't want to be reminded about not spending a lot of money — and certainly didn't want their friends and family to know they didn't spend a lot of money. Second, I now believe the niche that wanted us is much smaller than we thought. Third, I believe a niche looking to spend less will shop around and before you know it, they become so price conscious that they will take the lowest price over good service. The web just propels this effect. Even if you are pricing your product only 1% higher, you will be shopped and everyone will turn your product or service into a commodity. The race to the bottom begins and the chronic pain begins. This happens in a lot of industries. I experienced it in telecom and the web hosting business I owned. It was a lightning fast sprint to the bottom from competition across the world.

However, to be fair, the name was a shocker for the funeral business and got so much press it helped build the brand.

The point is: you don't need to reduce prices to absolutely smash the hell out of your competition, just create value. If you digitally transform, find cost savings, and turn that into value-added services giving your customers more bang for their buck, then, look out! You are going to steamroll everyone. This is much more effective than competing on price — and it will make it much more difficult for your competition to compete with you. Plus, it can provide a platform where you can upsell your customers. If you do it right.

So what is the overall financial benefit of the transformation when it's done right? That's the question every company wants to know before they start. When it comes to overall success of the transformation it can sometimes be as complex as an algorithm like Google's where there are countless parts that make up the successful sum. Modeling out all of those parts into hard dollars before you start becomes very difficult without some execution and a whole lot of testing. That's right—you need to take a calculated leap. When it works some call it Digital Transformation Magic, but experience tells me it's about the process of creating the ideas, implementing methodical testing, and launching with gusto — while measuring the financial benefits every moment.

So, in short, understanding your overall financial benefit requires a sober look at the current business model and a little bit of Wonder Theory as to what the potential might be. If you can't bring yourself to do something radical with the business, sometimes just a website overhaul can be an extremely effective toe in the water.

Let's take the socks off for a moment. I worked with a company that was very successful and they thought they were successful enough online and didn't need to worry about their website. Once we delved into their site stats, we uncovered that out of the 5,000 visitors per month, 80% of visitors left the site within 30 seconds — from the home page. (When someone leaves your site from the entrance page without interacting with the page, it's called a "bounce".) One might argue all of these visitors came to the site for a phone number and then left, but you'd have a better chance of winning the heavyweight championship of the world than finding a phone number on that site.

Here's how we helped them make a financial decision— if we improve the site with great automation, and make it easy for customers to dynamically interact in a flexible, fun way, could we possibly turn .5% of the 4,000 visitors the company didn't convert into customers? In this scenario they needed to decide if an extra 20 customers per month, or 240 customers per year, was worth it based on the overall cost of the website overhaul. For them, it was a no-brainer. Remember, all of these calculations were based on visitors they were already attracting and not crazy optimism about visitors they didn't have. If you took this simple website overhaul and went a few steps further and calculated that you could get an additional .5% through a Digital Transformation of the business model itself, you might have your answer on the financial viability. That is, as long as you knew what 480 new customers was worth to your company.

A Digital Transformation should always lead to a financial benefit and that must always be the main goal. Whether you sell for less (not your first option), or find a way to reduce internal costs, or increase your overall value proposition to smash your competition, profit is the goal to justify your Digital Transformation.

In the end, forecasts by their nature are usually wrong, but you need to do everything you can to crunch numbers to a point of mitigating your risk and turning it from a "throwing confetti in the air" decision into one that has been calculated.

*Caution: modeling is essential but you can't allow bean counting to kill the wonder required to take a calculated risk to succeed.*

## Cool-Fun

We talked about gamification. If you're not ready to take it as far as a game, if you are going to digitally transform, you might as well make it fun for your customers. Before I even start, I know there is someone out there saying, "I sell plumbing supplies, how the heck am I going to make that fun?"

OK, Mr. Plumbing Supply.

One thing I notice about plumbers is they always make multiple trips to Home Depot. No wonder they charge so much. What if you gave your customers a digital tool that allowed them to drag and drop pieces of pipes and fittings to create a schematic, or map of everything they need. And that would then output parts, numbers, measurements, delivery times, costs, and whatever else your customers need. Not only would that be helpful but it would feel like fun. Why the heck do you think puzzles sell so well? We've just come up with a time saving app that turns plumbing into a puzzle — that's a fun digital hook.

Don't limit yourself and say that there is no way to make something fun for your customers. If you think about our plumbing puzzle, how much time would it save plumbers and staff if they knew the exact part numbers and measurements for everything they would need before they started? The plumbing puzzle does this and would be a lot more fun for everyone. Functionality keeps people coming back again and again, and fun gets them talking — and posting, and sharing about it.

Sometimes it's not obvious how to digitally transform something like a manufactured product that has been around for years and make it fun. But there is always room for evolution if you commit to the transformation goal. Expose yourself to all the possibilities and try to crack the code on your transformation.

## DON'T MAKE THE TRANSFORMATION HOLLOW

Now that you know the Pillars, make sure they have substance and aren't hollow.

Back in the 1980's there was a mini-Renaissance in hot rod culture. It wasn't Fords and Chevys, it was VW's, Hondas, Toyotas, and Nissans. I worked construction all summer when I was 15 to get a car when I finally turned 16. A week after my 16th birthday I bought my first car, a Volkswagen Scirocco.

I loved that car. It had over 100,000 miles on it but it was mine, and the bank manager who owned it had totally "souped it up". Great performance, acceleration, and throaty sound that made you feel like you were driving a race car through a cavernous tunnel.

My buddy Randy had a VW GTI, and he was every teenage girl's father's worst nightmare. To this day he's still one of the funniest and craziest people I have ever met and also very successful. Back then, on the road, there was a VW family feud going between GTI's and Siroccos, and every time Randy got in my car, all he could talk about was the sound my car made.

So, Randy did what all the other guys did — he installed tips on his exhaust pipe and at 1:00 in the morning he'd wake up entire communities driving what sounded like a crippled race car. We all thought it was cool, but it didn't make his car any faster, it didn't make it handle better, and it sure didn't make it a Lamborghini. It was a hollow modification with hollow performance.

Your Wonder Theory, Revolution Delivery, Dynamic Interaction and Digital Hooks are no different. Your Digital Transformation has to be real and meaningful. I have spoken to so many business owners that just want to do something — anything. They think if they commit and believe they are going to be a huge success, then they will make a big splash.

I respect the attitude because it shows they know something needs to be done. However, all that energy has to translate into success. A gee-whiz model that doesn't increase sales or cut costs is a lot of gee without the whiz. An upgrade to an existing platform that makes it look better but perform worse is absolutely worthless. A calculator or any other digital hook on the site that isn't helpful is a distraction. An incredibly beautiful site that doesn't drive more sales is a disgrace. Never digitally transform without enough modelling to know your transformation strategy has substance, and the juice is worth the squeeze.

If you feel bad at this point because of misguided past failures, don't! We all have gone into something with so much passion we're blinded to the end result, but there is medication for that and it's called data. There is more data available than ever before that gives you a clear idea of how something will work before you start spending big dollars. You never could access it before. Now you can, and the kicker is — it's cheap.

I risk sounding like I'm repeating myself, but if you can't figure out an idea of what your customers want, how they want it, and where they want it, with the average costs of the transformation weighed against sales rates increased or expenses decreased through implementation of a plan or platform, then you are not ready to go. This is not to say a break-out-of-jail attitude is counter-productive, but bring that in after you have completed a thorough analysis of the data.

Once you have created your rock-star strategy and you are ready to implement, ask yourself the following questions:

- Is the Digital Transformation real?

- How much will this cost? Am I being realistic about my numbers?

- What are the soft costs? Will this disrupt my organization, or help it?

- How much is the return? Am I realistic about this number?

- Does this strategy require a change in staff I don't have? How do I find the staff I need?

- Is there something else that I should be doing for my business instead of this? (Another great thought from Ed Minich.) Sometimes there is bigger and easier bang for the buck than a Digital Transformation.

- Is the juice worth the squeeze — is the return worth the cost? Be bean-counter realistic because you have to have the numbers!

If this was too much explanation, think about this in dating terms. Your business can't risk a blind date. End of story.

# 8

# TRANSFORMATION OF WHAT WAS ALREADY DIGITAL

We've talked about Digital Transformation as a transformation of something that wasn't digital before. However, there are certain situations where a company that is already digital, or delivering a digital product or service, needs further transformation. Remember our definition:

*Digital Transformation is the deliberate and ongoing digital evolution of a company, business model, idea, process, or methodology, both strategically and tactically.*

Companies can't afford to be lazy anymore. We know this. Let's talk about some of the worst offenders in the digital world that are fighting the future.

## DIGITAL OFFENDERS!

I have lived in different states, different countries, and I can tell you that cable companies are dinosaurs wherever you go. They move slowly, their customers usually hate them and they seem to leverage their incumbency like extortionists instead of a platform to build loyalty. The Canadian cable companies are the worst digital offenders due to the lack of competition, while the US cable companies are much better but still far behind digitally transformed content delivery models. Let's look at the common cable model:

- They own the cable (known as the last mile) going to your house.

- They use that to deliver cable TV, internet and phone service.

- They usually have a wireless component to their business, i.e. cell phones, satellite.

In short, they deliver content. They are usually branded as communications companies but with no idea how to communicate. In fact, they are communication-inept companies and you've got to ask yourself, how did they get that way?

The first step to be communication-inept is, don't listen to the people you talk to — and I would say that is an overly fair statement when talking about the cable companies. How many people reading this book have tried to unbundle a channel package with your cable provider? They don't do it unless they are forced by the government. Making people pay for channels that they don't want is a very 20th century proposal. In fact, it's anti-digital. Digital and the web make it possible for us to get what we want, when we want, so if the cable companies aren't cooperating, then we are going to go out and get it for ourselves.

Do you have any idea how many movie and TV streaming services there are right now? Lots and lots, but let's talk about a couple of the titans. Hulu allows you to watch more TV than your brain could ever possibly process for $7.99 a month. Eight bucks and you get to watch every episode of TV shows in their current season. (For Canadian readers that are victim to some sort of evil plot by either the CRTC or some other regulatory body, you need to use a VPN service to make Hulu think you're in the USA.) Of course, we know iTunes has lots of TV shows and movies. Netflix is absolutely smashing everyone with almost 50+ million subscribers watching movies and TV shows. This is killing the cable companies, so the burning question is: why didn't the cable companies think of this in the first place? Why are they getting their clocks cleaned by a bunch of upstarts?

Any time a large incumbent considers a major change in their sales model that might reduce revenues or take revenues from existing business, the word "cannibalize" pops up. Remember what we said to do with those people? I would bet money that someone at

Blockbuster introduced the idea of streaming when they saw it coming and someone in the room started screaming about cannibalizing their precious stores. That person should have been sent to North Dakota to run a Blockbuster store.

If *you* are thinking about it, I promise you, your competition or a new upstart is thinking about it. The innovation might as well come from you and shutting down an idea because some fool in the room screams "cannibalization" is a luxury no longer allowed. The 80's are gone!

What's crazy is the phone and cable companies hold a tremendous amount of power. We invite them into our living rooms and they squander that by nickel and diming us to death. The easiest way to inspire a revolution is to make people feel like they are treated unfairly, and pick their pockets at the same time. And that is exactly what is happening. The phone and cable companies don't know how to transform their business models to the next level and, as a result, they are not giving us what we want.

The cable companies deliver digital content, and they are being smashed by digital models that deliver it ten times better, ten times cheaper. In fact, the Delivery Revolutionaries went one step further and deliver not only to your TV but to your computer and phone as well. All of this while the cable companies try to lock you into expensive packages with channels they should be paying you to watch. Sure the cable companies have on-demand service (clunky at best), but buying two movies through on-demand costs more than an entire month of Netflix. To make matters worse, once I start a movie I have to finish it in 48 hours, or I have to buy it again. This breaks one of the rules of Revolution Delivery because they are not giving me the product how I want it. Frustrating!

Remember I said they are not good at communication? I can't digitally connect with my cable provider to ask questions or contact support. Supposedly, my current cable company has online chat but when I called Support, it took a customer service rep over 3 minutes to find out where the chat button was. Chat, which is a standard for any company trying to serve and support customers on the web, is an absolute Easter egg hunt on my cable company's website. Such an excellent Easter egg hunt, their own reps couldn't find it.

So, what is the phone and cable companies' response to getting smashed by their lack of innovation and Digital Transformation? They start tracking usage to charge customers for more internet bandwidth. Rather than penalize customers for what is inevitable, they need to figure out how to keep these customers because low-cost service providers are popping up, and the phone and cable companies are being forced to give them access over their lines. Titans like Verizon will continue to do well with their internet and wireless businesses but, all in all, these digital companies are not digitally transforming — they're starting a long term process leading to their deaths or, at the least, their contraction.

All of these reasons are why people are jumping ship to companies like Amazon, Hulu and Netflix, because they are benefitting from one of the four pillars of Digital Transformation — Revolution Delivery. And at this moment, this stage of development of the web and our global economy, offering even a single pillar like Revolution Delivery can be a powerful Digital Transformation.

But it is not just the phone and cable companies. I have a PlayStation for my kids and that's how we watch Netflix because it has a built-in Netflix App. You would think that Sony would want to take advantage of having almost 80 million consoles sitting in living rooms around the world. To be clear, I am not privy to the Netflix/ PlayStation deal but Sony has their device sitting in all these living rooms and its own PlayStation Store where you can rent movies. Unfortunately, I tried the Sony service and found it clunky and half-baked — another example of another giant allowing upstarts to run away with a nice chunk of recurring revenue on their platform. When I say nice chunk, I mean a nice chunk, because Netflix has gross margins of 28%.

However, we do need to give it up to Sony because they could identify Netflix was going to be a very important player and understood the need to partner with them. They made a deal with Amazon as well. However, you would think someone in Sony could make it easier to deal with Sony. Unfortunately, bloated decision-making processes in large corporations lead us to believe it was easier to make deals with outside players than with themselves.

## Digital trailblazer gets lazy & out-transformed

So far we have talked about businesses that need to go through an initial Digital Transformation, but what happens when you don't continue to digitally evolve after you transform? Let's look at a company that digitally transformed an entire industry but stopped. This company got complacent while someone else was creating their own incredible transformation event. Let's finally smash this berry for everything it's worth, and serve it up at a smartphone breakfast.

We already talked about it, but let's think about this heartbreak at a different angle for a moment. Initially, Blackberry crushed the regular cell phone market and they were riding higher than high. Businesses around the world were crazy for Blackberry, and Blackberry were selling phones like Vulcan ears at a Star Trek Convention. Blackberry was the ever-loving poster child of Digital Transformation. Then, all of a sudden, Apple came out of nowhere with a phone that absolutely changed everything.

Yep, the touchscreen, the apps, the ease, and Blackberry ignoring the consumer market—to me this is just details. The important part of the story is Blackberry quit evolving. By the time the iPhone released in June of 2007 the Blackberry was already a modern dinosaur, because they stopped asking themselves the most important question: "What do my customers want tomorrow?" That is the fundamental question of Digital Transformation and, if Blackberry had kept asking that, they would have evolved.

Blackberry thought that everyone would want a phone that had a tactile keyboard that made up for a terrible browser experience and no apps, because they were on top of the world. They didn't get what is important to people and they still don't. If you've been paying attention Blackberry has a new CEO that looks as lost as the last one. He recently bashed the rest of the smartphone market saying the smartphones on the market had crappy batteries. His PR people must have come up with the phrase "wall huggers," because that's his new put-down for people who need to charge their batteries all the time and his rationale for why people would put up with an inferior Blackberry experience. What he doesn't realize is that all the Blackberry users are hugging the wall with their laptops because they can't do anything with their Blackberry. Hell, they are even going to have a hard time holding the new Passport as it resembles a paving stone.

This is not to say that Blackberry doesn't have some positive things going for it but, as a former user, it would be nice to see them get their act together. Stopping the denial would be a good start. I would (almost) waive my fee to sit with that executive team and engage in a serious "Suck Session" and then a little Wonder Theory.

Of course, Apple has been fantastic at asking what customers want tomorrow but I think they have stopped asking that question recently, or stopped listening to the answer. They're starting to look like a clunky proprietary product. That is why Android is starting to smash them. Android is in touch with the social consciousness of their customers and the fact people want an easy mobile experience they can customize and make their own. My prediction, and I do hate putting myself on the line with this, is Apple is going to hiccup a bit.

Remember, just because you have transformed and conquered the world doesn't mean you can stop for even a moment and marvel at your success. Competition is around the corner. Look at history for a lesson on how a mighty empire can fall. The Roman Empire wasn't destroyed by one enemy in one battle. Instead, its empire was picked apart by enemies and battles within and without, over time. Let's give you the tools to be the conqueror instead of the conquered.

# 9

## THE FALLACY OF THE NEW IDEA

### TRANSFORMATION IN ALL THE RIGHT PLACES

How many times has someone told you they have a great idea for a business? How many times has someone told you their idea has never been done before? How many times has someone told you they have come up with something totally new? With the amount of times I hear this on a daily basis you would think that they were putting entrepreneur drugs in our water.

What I've come to realize is there are very few *new* ideas out there. At this point in our evolution of both the world and the business world, trying to find a pure new idea is about as common as sending someone to space. In other words, it happens very rarely.

I am all about entrepreneurial spirit, and there is nothing that gets me more charged up than hearing a great business idea, but this isn't the early 1900's. We are living in a world where it's hard to hear a song that doesn't feel recycled. Hard to find a movie that doesn't remind us of something else. In fact, our generations relate to whatever is new with something from the past. I'm not a Lady Gaga fan but when I see her all I think of is Madonna mixed with Elton John and it doesn't seem groundbreaking to me.

Business is not that much different. The last time we had a really new idea was the computer. If you think about it, there was nothing like the computer before there was a computer, nothing like a car before a car, and nothing like a television before a television. Airplane ... same thing.

Instead of looking at opportunities as new ideas, we need to look at them for what they usually are: better execution, or borrowed execution. Almost every business and product we use falls into these two different groups. Innovations and improvements of these things can be great ideas. All I'm saying is they're not exactly new ideas.

## BETTER EXECUTION

This one is easy as the majority of businesses that have transformed, and industries that have digitally transformed, have been all about better execution.

Facebook is probably the most famous example as it was a better execution of Myspace's model. EBay immediately comes to mind since they combined the auction idea, which has been around for thousands of years, and took selling your stuff in garage sales, classified ads, and with posters on telephone poles, and bundled it into a nice clean digital auction. Was the idea brilliant? Maybe, but it was better execution and their timing was even better. We were ready for it and it was better execution for anyone selling something. eBay then evolved the used car sales/salesman process until even used car salesman threw their hands up in a "If you can't beat 'em, join 'em" moment and started using eBay themselves.

We're surrounded by better execution — think of Evernote: better execution for taking notes either on paper or even simple note apps; Eventbrite: better execution on an event planner; Amazon: better execution buying books (and now everything else); LinkedIn: better execution on a Rolodex; iTunes: better execution delivering music (however, they are going to be out-transformed by streaming music unless they move quickly).

eBay didn't come up with the auction idea, Amazon wasn't the first one to sell books, Netflix wasn't the first to rent movies, and iTunes wasn't the first to sell music and Evernote sure wasn't the first one to come up with taking notes or sharing them with your devices, they just put it all together. What these companies did was take what was already out there and execute one million times better. When you think about it that way, it doesn't feel as groundbreaking as these companies appear to be.

Never, ever, underestimate the power of better execution. If you stop for a minute and look around, you will see there are better execution opportunities everywhere. This is one of the main things I do in business and it is the product of a digitally-tuned brain. Better execution is Digital Transformation incarnate. I bet you, right now, if you take a moment, get your Wonder Theory going, and look at your business and industry, you will find the gem that is better execution. I transformed an entire industry doing just that, and you can too.

## BORROWED EXECUTION

This is not a new concept, and it is not necessarily a business model. People borrow thoughts, ideas, processes and philosophies from different places, times and cultures all the time. It happens constantly in sports. Someone comes up with a new training routine, diet, or supplement, and suddenly everyone is doing it. I remember in high school the football players participated in wrestling practice to see how we trained, because pound for pound we were in the best shape around. They took that onto the football field and absolutely smashed their competition. Business is no different.

All kinds of businesses pop up that borrow execution from other industries. Let's start nice and easy. I have talked a lot about streaming video in this book, but at the time of this writing there is a lot of talk about streaming music. YouTube Music is rumored to be coming and there is another service called Beats Music getting a lot of attention. To my eyes, this is just borrowed execution from something that already works — internet radio. Internet radio has been around for a long time but listening to what you want, when you want, is what makes these new options different. Do I hear Revolution Delivery? However, the danger here is that most songs are already on YouTube, so it will be interesting to see if there is any traction there.

I've already described how I digitally transformed the funeral industry — but the quote building system, real-time chat and online submission were nothing new. Sure, we tweaked the concept like crazy through a ton of heavy lifting and the result was better execution overall but, in the end, lots of it was borrowed. Borrowed execution is all around and if you pay attention to it you'll notice lots of the things you like are clearly borrowed. In fact, your smartphone is borrowed execution—computer and phone.

Sometimes borrowed execution is mixed with better execution and you see this a lot with bricks and mortar models online. If you look at Forbes' current list of America's Most Promising Companies, you'll find borrowed, better and mixed execution all over the place. One of the more shining examples is Craftsy which is really your local community center classes, online. Quilting, cooking, painting, sewing, gardening — everything craftsy. A groundbreaking new idea? No, but it's borrowed execution from all the online universities that don't offer these types of classes.

Borrow, borrow, borrow ... and borrow some more. In the business world this is just another way to say "best practices". Some of the best, best practices are the ones taken from other industries. Do whatever it takes to get to a point where you pull from everyone and everywhere. Stop reading and think about what you can borrow or better in your industry. Constant evolution doesn't necessarily mean you have to be new to be smart. Just smart enough to know what's smart.

# 10

# THE RIGHT INGREDIENTS

A t this point you may be thinking you are not ready for Digital Transformation. If I was in front of you, I would tape a ringing alarm clock around your head and tell you to wake up and live the Wonder Theory. To help, I am going to show you what I have experienced as the right ingredients for Digital Transformation. There are no hard and fast rules, so there's no excuse if your business doesn't fit into these. Get a little Chef Ramsey without all the angst and F-Bombs and make the recipe to transform your business — but you are going to need these ingredients.

Once in a while, I meet what I call a dream leader. A dream leader is someone who, first and foremost, is not in denial and, second, is open to a new vision. A dream leader I helped, let's call him Jack, was that guy and much more. He's an icon in his industry and although he is known for his artistic attributes, he is a shrewd businessman. He came to me because he had a well-established business that kicked out a ton of revenue but not a lot of profit, because he only utilized 60% of his total capacity while carrying 100% of the costs. Jack knew his business was feeling antiquated and asked me how I would digitally transform it to cut costs and drive revenue. Once we engaged and sat down to examine what was going on, I knew I had a dream leader on my hands. Jack had everything we needed to digitally transform his business.

In my experience, the right ingredients a business needs for Digital Transformation are:

- Digital Strategy and Planned Execution
- People
- Product
- Industry
- Social Temperature

Some of these look familiar because they are important in many aspects of business but we are going to look at this from a transformation perspective. Let's break them down one by one for Jack's business.

## DIGITAL STRATEGY AND PLANNED EXECUTION

This is a no-brainer because Digital Transformation without a Strategic Plan is suicide. After diving deep into Wonder Theory you need to have a clear and concise strategy about what you are going to do and planned execution describing how you are going to do it. Planning has been beaten into our heads forever, but planned execution doesn't happen enough. Within a second, the execution of a Digital Transformation can fall off the rails, and it happens in the most innocent way.

Transformation is exciting and, when people get excited, there are more and more ideas. During a transformation you or someone on your team is going to say, "Hey, let's do this too!" and then someone else will say, "Hey, I just came up with something and let's do this as well!" Before you know it, there are so many ideas and plans going on that the initial plan is overwhelmed and then one of two things happens:

1. Your Digital Transformation ends up crashing and burning and you sit in the ashes wondering what the heck just happened.

2. You're so overwhelmed with all the different directions you don't execute anything.

Either way your execution has gone off like a bottle rocket and exploded into nothing and with it, your Digital Transformation. You should never stop listening to or logging the ideas but when it comes to execution, stick with the plan because there will always be time to tweak or add on after.

Jack didn't have that problem because we had a rock-solid Digital Strategy and execution plan. When I say rock solid, I mean the plan was clear, concise, and in writing. (Lots of plans are not in writing and that's like letting your 16 year old practice stick shift in your Porsche. Lots of grinding while trying to move forward.) There were no questions about the goals and what needed to be done to execute. In addition, Jack had expert project management so falling off the rails wasn't going to happen. The execution went according to plan. The first rule is planned execution — do not start without it.

A good starting point for this first Digital Transformation ingredient are to answer the following questions:

- Who are we trying to sell to? (This should be so detailed that you could almost create an avatar.)

- What are we trying to sell or deliver digitally? (This may be different from what you are currently offering.)

- How we are going to embrace Revolution Delivery to give our customers what they want and make it simple for them to buy?

- How will we dynamically interact with our customers?

- Are there ways that we can better execute or borrow execution?

- What is the financial justification for doing this?

- Do we have the personnel/resources to execute? If so, who?

- What are the steps and timelines to execute?

- Is this the best thing that we could or should be doing right now for our business?

Once that is done then you can take this information and use it to create a Digital Strategy. Though this is extremely high level, the components of a Digital Strategy should be the following:
- Website
  - Design/Function/Messaging

- o Digital Hooks/Content
- o Conversion/Sale Event
- Sales & Operations
  - o Sales
  - o Supply Chain
  - o Customer Service
  - o Delivery
- Digital Marketing Strategy
  - o Network Display/Real Time Bidding (RTB)/Mobile
  - o Facebook/LinkedIn
  - o Content/Landers/Banners
  - o Retargeting
- Social Media Strategy
  - o FB/Twitter/Instagram
  - o Google+/LinkedIn/YouTube
  - o Content
  - o Podcasting
- Leadership Casting
  - o Content
  - o PR
  - o Article Submission
- Financial
  - o Financial Benefits
- Revenue Generation
- Cost Savings
  - o Acquisition Metrics
  - o Revenue to Profit

You can see this visually in Figure 2 and notice that it is circular. If you take a good look at this, you will most likely find a hole or multiple holes in your Digital Strategy. In fact, you might find that you only have a website and don't have a Digital Strategy at all. Get crackin'! Once you have all of this, then you can bang out a solid plan for execution. I am not going to go through all of the components of an execution plan, but they don't call it project management for nothing. Make sure your project is managed by someone who has the tools to get it done.

*Figure 2 – Digital Strategy*

## People

Jack was totally game for evolving and transforming his business, but it added a lot of horsepower that his general manager in charge of operations was also excited about the prospect. He completely bought into our overall vision, and believed it was critical for the long-term survival of the business. Jack's other confidants within the business also shared his enthusiasm.

I remember Jack brought in his PR agent on our second meeting because he knew the Digital Transformation of his business was going to be newsworthy. He loved the vision for transformation and ran with it. When you Digitally Transform, it inspires everyone around you and creates a culture that pays dividends. Inspiring your people pays off big time. The more you nurture the transformation culture by involving everyone who cares about the business, the more the momentum will grow. All of this momentum boosts morale, and in the end will boost revenues and profits. From an IT perspective Jack didn't really have an IT team but he didn't need one, as the solutions were web based. Outsourced development and management was easy and cost effective.

In essence, the people that made up the senior team were in place, focused, and ready for transformation. Jack's employees were also really excited about it. Most of them were young enough that the digital image of the business meant something to them personally. They were behind the strategy 100%. When it came to the "people ingredient" Jack had the total package to digitally transform his business.

Digital Transformation is not reserved for big companies alone. No matter what the size of the company, it should always be digitally evolving. There are plenty of companies out there with only 5-10 employees that can and should digitally transform. Even these companies can gather the resources either inside or outside the company to make a transformation. In fact, I recently spent time with a company that had nine employees and it was obvious they needed a Digital Transformation. The company was very profitable but they had hit a revenue ceiling under their current model. The need for Digital Transformation was obvious and it was in reach.

## PRODUCT

Jack's business had a few subsidiaries and none of them were selling anything online, because everyone thought they couldn't. However, Jack had incredible products and they were a fantastic foundation to build on. I can hear some of you saying, "Well, of course you have to have great products." I could reply that great marketing can sell anything, but you're right. You have to have a great product AND great marketing to transform an industry. But, almost any product can appear great — it's how you brand it, and sell it, to the right target market. With the funeral business we didn't have a better product than anyone else — it was how we marketed and sold it.

For Jack, we came up with a different way to sell his products and services online. When I broached the subject with Jack his face lit up because he saw the potential right away. For the first time, Jack realized his local business could go global and by taking his brand around the world it could generate an exciting new source of revenue. The right products put us in a position for massive sales once we digitally transform.

*Attention doubting reader: Don't tell yourself that your products or services cannot be sold digitally. Everything can and should be sold digitally. If you have something that is extremely difficult to sell, all the better because the digital format lets you explain it with all kinds of assistance like video, animated video, infographics, web tools, quote builders, and whatever else you can come up with.*

## INDUSTRY

You don't have to revolutionize an industry to digitally transform your business, but certain industries are ripe to have the proverbial box smashed, so you might as well go for it. Not to mention transforming an industry is a heck of a lot more fun than you can imagine. It's fact — certain industries are too comfortable and have done the same thing for so long that, if you digitally transform your business, you not only get a leg up, you'll smash the entire industry.

Jack's industry wasn't that technically savvy even though his customers were. Before his Digital Transformation there were definitely some competitors ahead of Jack but 97% of them weren't. Jack was what I would call a medium-size player in the industry. There weren't a lot of giants around and they weren't a threat as his business catered to a higher-end customer base. It was all the little guys who were eating his lunch one chip at a time.

Jack's industry was ripe for Digital Transformation and it was going to help him gain market share from the little guys and entice some of the customer base from the giants. The real beauty of this was that many of the little guys were distribution clients of his and one of the platforms we put together allowed him to distribute some of his technology to them for an ongoing monthly fee. This generated recurring revenue out of his competitors while keeping a bit of control over them via the technology. Check and mate. Jack transformed his industry and did it with a smile by sharing some of that Digital Transformation for a nice monthly fee!

## SOCIAL TEMPERATURE

It's well known in business that the first market mover can be successful, but it's less well known that the second market mover is often the one who cashes in. This happens because the first trailblazer has paved the way and prepared people for what the second market mover is offering. Those first market movers go through all kinds of business hell because it takes a tremendous amount of effort to warm up an audience. I experienced this personally with Basic Funerals. There were lots of people absolutely opposed to the idea of arranging their funerals online. However, now it's not so new, and people are open to doing it — more so with every additional competitor entering the market, and I can tell you there are a lot of them.

Jack's customer base was completely web savvy as they were a younger demographic. Consequently, the social temperature was just right to digitally transform his business model. He could be a first market mover, and his customers wouldn't hesitate to gobble up what he had to offer. The social temperature has to be there for Digital Transformation to really work.

One of the questions you might be asking is, "If you don't have social temperature, is the idea of a Digital Transformation dead in the water?" Absolutely not! All that means is you are going to need to be a very savvy marketer and communicator. You are going to have to create a bit of the ground swell that gets people talking about your company and products, and how you do things differently.

There are so many different ways to do this, and it depends on whether you have a B2B or B2C business. A B2C business can kick up all kinds of interest through social means and great public relations. A bit tougher with a B2B business but great PR never hurt anyone. If you don't have social temperature, find a great PR agent that is excited about what you're doing and hire them. PR can do wonders. I am in good company with this line of thinking. Jim McCaan, the founder of 1-800-Flowers who transformed the flower business told me that, without a doubt, he would trade all of the advertising in the world for PR. I second that motion!

Remember, great social temperature is a must and it can be created. If I look back at all of my business experiences, creating social temperature was probably one of the most enjoyable parts of building a business and transforming an industry—difficult as hell, but fun.

I repeat — you don't have to have all of these ingredients to get it right, but you have to have some of them. You must absolutely have the right people. If you don't have them, hire them. If you can't hire them, bring in a hired gun for a short amount of time, but don't try it without them. Something like social temperature varies so don't give yourself a lame excuse to delay because of that.

Again and again, I will say it. You need to get going now and if you don't have the right ingredients go out and get them and put them together piece by piece! It's important to get the process going, because all of this takes time to prepare and simmer and every day is revenue, market share and opportunity lost. Go, Go, Go!

*The next two sections are not ingredients, but two things to keep in mind while transforming.*

## TRANSFORMING FOR THE MASSES

The whole world has gone into a tailspin about niches. Niche your product, niche your market, niche a segment of the market, niche, niche, niche. What they don't tell you about is all the failed niche businesses.

No matter how big a market is, it has a finite size and a finite number of buyers. When you transform your company, make sure you do it with the masses in mind. Transform the market and all the niches underneath. Sure some things are better specialized but if you're going to transform, throw a bomb instead of a firecracker. When you spend time contemplating your transformation, and you think about what people want or don't want, always think about the common denominator.

This is really a common sense strategy because you want to sell the most products or services to the most people. It's that simple. Again, niching is great when it comes to trying to pick off your place in the market, but mastering the market and all the niches underneath it should be a digital goal. The digital portion helps make transforming for the masses possible. Put some Wonder Theory to work on that and see what you find. Yes, that's actually the end of this section. Enough said!

### Transform for the Tab

Another consideration when transforming for the masses are devices and platforms. It doesn't matter what product or service you sell, or if it is B2B or B2C, you have to consider the mobile/tablet market. If you haven't yet, don't feel bad, you're not alone. Most people still build their digital strategy based on the illusion people use either a PC or Mac — but that of course is no longer the case. The desktop computer is becoming an afterthought and, now that you know, you can no longer plead digital stupid.

You might sit there thinking, what does this have to do with anything? You can pull up your site on a phone or tablet easily. That may be the case, but how does it look and how does it perform converting visitors into sales? If your site is not tablet or mobile-ready, and it is not 100% easy to use on these devices, then you are going to lose customers. You absolutely have to make sure you build your digital strategy and overall transformation with this in mind. Whether it is a site, an app, a model, an offer, a product … anything. Mobile and tablet will rule the world shortly, so make sure you don't put yourself behind a desktop wall. Keep the growing mobile audience in mind.

Most people don't realize mobile marketing is a bit of a different beast than digital marketing. Mobile marketing is growing like crazy and unless you and your business are mobile-ready you aren't going to benefit. You need to have a mobile platform that converts visitors into sales and please understand that this is done very differently compared to your desktop site. If all of that wasn't enough, the world of wearable devices like Google Glass and a whole mountain of things to come will need to be a future consideration. Barron's cited a Credit Suisse analyst in 2013 that stated wearables are going to be "the next big thing" and is forecasting that the market will ramp from approximately $3B-$5B today to $50 billion in the next 3-5 years. That is a lot of wearable tech and I imagine we will all feel like we are living in a non-stop Star Trek convention. We can't be sure how accurate that Credit Suisse forecast will be, but it will definitely be something to think about when you continue to digitally evolve in the future.

To close on this point, always, always, always transform for the masses. Take a look at your client base and the segment that brings the most money, combine that with a larger target for the masses, and build your strategy in that direction. And while you're doing it make sure you consider the rapidly expanding mobile audience, so you capture them too.

# 11

## WHY TRANSFORMATION WORKS

### OH YEAH! YOU'RE DOING THIS TO PROFIT

Now I hope I've got you warmed up by telling you some of the success stories of businesses that Digitally Transform and some of the horror stories of those that didn't. You know the four pillars and you know the ingredients. However, you still may not understand why the heck you are doing this, and why it will work.

You are doing this to grow your business and it all boils down to one thing — profit. You need to get your customers to have a Dynamic Interaction with your business through Digital Hooks, Revolution Delivery, and the right cost model, which will entice them into a sales conversion process that generates profit. Remember, profit is the absolute #1 goal, and you need sales to generate revenue in a cost-effective way to generate profit. You need a model that works, and does so consistently 24/7/365. That's why you're doing it. However, you still might need to understand why it works or believe that it does. If you still don't believe in what I am telling you and you're coming up with all kinds of excuses, then you are snow blind to what I call the Christmas effect.

### THE CHRISTMAS EFFECT

I don't care what religion you are, everyone likes getting gifts, and Christmas is a great excuse for that. Think about it — what do we like about Christmas gifts? We love the anticipation. We love the feeling something is coming. But what we really love is knowing there is a present wrapped up just for us. We love that — someone giving us something special, just for us, and we get to unwrap it.

Have you ever noticed when someone gives an intangible gift, no matter how big it is — a trip, concert, spa treatment, whatever -- they like to give a little something as well, like a card, because they think, "I have to get them something they can open on Christmas Day"? WE LOVE OPENING PRESENTS, and that is a powerful emotion you can't ignore. It's WHY PEOPLE LOVE BUYING ONLINE.

When we buy online, we get excited about getting it in our hands and we can't wait for the mailman to bring our purchase. We're like kids on Christmas morning waiting to open our Christmas presents. We experience all kinds of emotions like anticipation, excitement, and of course, gratification — the arrival of a packaged present we bought. Buying online has all the attributes of Christmas except it can happen all year long and we pay for our presents. I call that the Christmas Effect.

If you have a business, and people actually come *to you* to get your product/service, you need to rethink your model ASAP to go *to them*. If you sell industrial cranes that's a different story but most products can be shipped by mail. Amazon gets the Christmas effect and it's common knowledge they made a deal with the US Postal Service (USPS) for Sunday deliveries in select cities, and plans to expand that. The Canadian Postal Service has completely shifted its focus to service online business.

Think about that — Amazon has done what millions of businesses over 50 years have been unable to do — they got the USPS to open their doors on Sunday. Because Amazon knows people want their purchases right now or they will suffer going to Wal-Mart if they have to. Amazon has made itself one of the most powerful retailers on Earth, because they know if you purchase something on a Friday night you want it NOW. And when you're a titan like Amazon it might just be delivered to you while you're in your robe and fuzzy slippers on Sunday. That is the Christmas Effect, 7 days a week, and that is power.

Amazon is, of course, trying to take this one step further with the unmanned aerial vehicle (UAV) delivery service they are trying to launch called Prime Delivery. If you haven't seen the slick commercial Amazon has put together, you should. You buy something, it gets loaded onto a UAV and is flown to your house the same day you purchase it. How long it will take to work through the government red tape is an unknown, but it's Amazon and I wouldn't bet against them. That is the Christmas Effect, 24 hours a day, 7 days a week, and that is even more powerful.

Others will follow and are in the process of doing so, but the lesson is, online retailers are taking advantage of the Christmas Effect. They flex to accommodate their customers, make it easy to shop and constantly push to deliver those little presents quicker. Amazon is at the forefront of understanding and creating the Christmas Effect because it constantly digitally transforms. They never wait for the competition to innovate before they do. Amazon is the king of the Christmas Effect because they know they aren't perfect and constantly ask themselves, "Why does Amazon Suck?" "Why wouldn't we buy from Amazon?" The answer was most likely, that instant gratification sells, and to be successful they needed to tackle this issue. Which they continue to do — constantly.

Once upon a time, Amazon only sold books and only delivered books. When e-books started, did they worry about cannibalizing the fulfillment and delivery of their base model? Absolutely not. They knew the power of instant gratification. Even when a package isn't delivered through the mail, the instant gratification when you download your e-book is enough to create a virtual Christmas Effect.

The biggest reason we bite the bullet and buy things in stores for higher prices is we want them now! Amazon saw the future and went for it by lighting up Kindle and crushing the e-Book market. Then, they figured out a lot of people like to listen to books instead of reading them, so they bought Audible in 2008 (books are even easier now because we don't have to read them). Did they worry about people not buying their books after listening to them? Do they care? I don't think so. They are reaping the profits no matter what, and they keep moving, and moving, and moving forward. They never stop. This is not just a digital transformation but full business transformation on a consistent basis.

All of this holds true for B2B businesses because businesspeople are people too.

We talked about products in this environment, now let's talk about services. The Christmas Effect is valid for the service world as well. The big problem selling a service is it's difficult to get your hands around something you can't hold. When you buy a product online you know at some point you will get something you can hold. The real magic is if you can deliver that tangible feeling by selling something online that isn't tangible.

This is why apps are so successful. When you think about it, apps are only software and graphics, but your phone or tablet gives you a tactile experience — so it feels real. If you sell your service on your website, and your only strategy is to tell them about your service, there's nothing a potential customer can hold. You need to package it for them. When I say package, you need to put something on the web that looks and feels like a package — an experience they can hold.

In some of my past businesses, I underestimated the power of packaging and ran them a la carte. But what we didn't realize was people wanted packages, at least visual ones. I realized that even though we were providing a service, we needed something that looked like a physical object on the website, something you could get your hands around with a price attached. One of my managers was a doubter. He was smart and analytical, but he always wanted to be the smartest guy in the room and loved to challenge the boss (me). He said, "That's not going to make a difference." I said, "Get it done and let's look at the numbers." Of course it made a difference. People finally had something visual and psychologically they felt get they could get their hands around it. That was enough to bump up the conversions and bring down the bounce rate.

Take your cue from well-designed sites on the web, ones that know how to sell, that package their items conceptually and visually. You should ask yourself, "Do I make it easy for customers to do business with me? Do they enjoy it as much as possible? Do I deliver my product in a satisfying way? Do I give them instant gratification? Am I generating the Christmas Effect? "

The technology is out there and all you have to do is use it to your advantage to make your sales process satisfying. Remember the Christmas effect. If you can make the process of buying something on your site feel like Christmas, then customers are going to sit in your virtual lap and ask you for everything they want.

## THE STRAWBERRY MODEL

One summer, when I was 17, my buddy Andreas and I decided we didn't want typical summer jobs and we were going to work for ourselves. After working construction for two straight summers I really didn't feel like killing myself for $6 an hour again. So, we decided to start a business.

Andreas's dad was the Greek Tycoon of the produce business, and I used to help deliver on occasion. We thought about opening a produce business, but we realized we didn't have the money or the credit to make a go of that. Then, we thought, everyone loves strawberries, maybe we could buy strawberries from a distributor and sell them to restaurants. We did, but by the end of the first day we realized the margins were pretty thin, and we weren't going to make enough money to pay for our gas and go out to the clubs that night. How could we get this going and actually make some money? We got smart and went straight to the farmer.

A big tough Japanese guy ran this big strawberry farm about 30 minutes away, which we were pretty sure was just a front for the Japanese Yakuza. He was tough but we made a great deal with him and cut our costs by more than half. Every morning we would fill our cars up with cases of strawberries and pound the pavement selling them to businesses door to door. This was one of my first forays into cold calling and I have to tell you, at 17, we had brass balls. We just marched in and started selling our strawberries.

My strawberry business taught me one of the most important pieces of my Digital Transformation toolkit. If you make things easy for people and you put it right in front of them, they will buy. That summer was probably the first time those businesses had someone walk in their door with strawberries for sale. Even though they weren't thinking about strawberries, they didn't have to exert themselves to purchase. That on its own sold almost 50% of our product because when people like it and you make it easy, they will buy.

We had confirmed our supply line because we had a direct

relationship with the farm; we could undercut the grocery stores if we wanted but cost wasn't a factor because we sold on ease of purchase and freshness; and we picked a product people would love. The sales proposition wouldn't have been nearly as compelling with Brussels sprouts.

Part of the reason we did so well back then was our relentless marketing style. This style is also why digital marketing is so effective at bringing in customers. We kept putting the option in front of people and would often go into the same places, even if they said no the first time, because eventually it was the right time and they would buy our strawberries. Digital marketing accomplishes the same thing without the work and the expense. When that customer is finally interested don't worry, they'll click, but until that happens you don't pay a dime.

We're lucky to live in a world of ever-growing choices and options, but sometimes the environment needs to be just right to make a sale. When you put the right product in front of the right customer, with the right pitch, the right number of times, you are going to eventually close them. And once this process starts you will start optimizing the steps to make a better, faster sale more often. Take a look at Figure 3 to see what I'm talking about. Andreas and I became very practiced at our pitch and had learned the right places to walk into. One of our hottest target markets turned out to be hair salons as both stylists and clients would buy cartons of strawberries like crazy.

It was our only job that summer and we had a great time doing it. We learned how to cut out the middleman, find the right product, the right target market, the right pitch, and sell our product on a consistent basis. Although we didn't know it at the time, we put ourselves through an early process of optimization.

This can be directly translated for any business and become your path for success, and Digital Transformation makes it that much easier. Your model for success is, build an evolutionary model, a great website, create digital hooks, a digital sales funnel, an e-commerce platform, and use a digital marketing strategy to put the right products in front of the right customer at the right time. If you do this correctly the strategy works. It's a no-brainer. Don't be overwhelmed by all the things you have to do, and don't get discouraged during the beginning phases of getting your digital engine rolling. Just break it down and ask yourself, "Am I putting the right strawberries in front of the right people the right way, the right amount of times?" When you finally get to say, "Yes," get ready for the tidal wave of business coming your way.

## STRAWBERRY MODEL

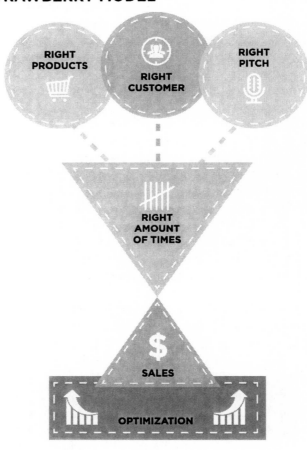

*Figure 3 – Strawberry Model*

# 12
# GETTING YOUR COMPANY READY

By now, I hope you have a better understanding of Digital Transformation, and Wonder Theory is igniting your brain. The next phase is to figure out how to make all this happen. Your first step is getting the people in your company behind it. Here are a few methods I have seen work.

## MAKE IT A REAL POSITION IN THE COMPANY

Do you know that right now at the time of this writing there are over 2000 jobs on LinkedIn alone that have to do with digital? V.P. of Digital Strategy, Director of Digital Strategy, Digital Marketing strategists, Digital Content strategists. If you haven't been paying attention, these are the positions that progressive companies that don't want to die are looking for and so should you. Start your search by announcing to your staff that you have created a new position and anyone in the company can apply for it — Director or Manager of Digital Transformation. Part of the application process should include how they would digitally transform something as un-transformable as, say, "hats," and how they would digitally transform your company. Make it into a position and tell the entire company this is a serious initiative. People will talk. You might have a rock star that's been quietly looking at your issues, and hasn't said a word. Or, you might have someone inside the company with an incredible entrepreneurial spirit, who may even have a digital side business going, and they really understand the digital world.

Large Corporations can be career black holes. They're not very good identifying who is great and who is not, usually because many direct managers act as gatekeepers. When I was at Bell, the job was amazing at the start. I dealt with five Fortune 500 companies and managed over $200 million of business during my tenure. I took care of everything from closing large deals and negotiating contracts to wining and dining C-Level execs. I always blew my numbers out of the water and I started looking for more ways to flex my creative side. Ma Bell made clear she was not going to allow that. She didn't want to give a guy that was bringing in millions of dollars of business another role because that is where I was slotted.

So, I left. I started 3 businesses, and bought another one. Could I have helped Bell digitally transform? Probably better than most people in the company because how many of their Canadian employees owned a web-hosting company in the USA with thousands of customers? Do you think if they had created a position calling for a creative and strategic thinker who understood the digital world, I would have applied? Absolutely. Were there other people lurking in the company with great ideas and great skills? Absolutely. If they put out a companywide survey asking for suggestions would I have done that? Nope, no way, no how. Waste of time, no money, and no credit for that.

Don't turn Digital Transformation into a project, turn it into an opportunity. Digital Transformation is a big job and it may be a cost center at the start but it will be a profit center by the end. Turn it into a high profile position and you'll get high profile results.

Let's look at another option.

## MAKE IT A CULTURE

As I mentioned earlier, I was a professional musician, and I'm sure it's one of the fundamental reasons my brain is wired abnormally. I played stand-up bass and learned a lot playing music and playing all different kinds of music, but most of the time I was a jazz snob. Jazz is a highly sophisticated art form based on what is called structured improvisation. That means, you need to create on a second-by-second basis, and that reprograms your mind. It's a tight knit culture and I didn't even realize I was a part of it. Every moment, I was completely engrossed in the music. I played, thought or talked about music all day, all night. I was completely immersed in the culture of playing jazz music. I wasn't making tons of money but I would have done anything for the music because I felt like I was doing something that was bigger than me. And the reason I felt that way was that every night four other musicians counted on me to be the absolute best I could and, then, to be better even than that. It was part of the culture.

What if you did that for your company? What if you created a culture of Digital Transformation? What if every single person in the company thought about Digital Transformation morning and night? What if all anyone talked about was digitally transforming parts or all of your company? What if everyone got some personal enjoyment out of it? What if they could derive satisfaction from coming up with a great idea about transforming the company? What if it was constant because innovative thinking was rewarded and not held back by a gatekeeper? That is the power of creating a Digital Transformation culture. Plus, it raises the overall culture of the company to a new level because everyone is involved.

You might ask why I stopped playing music if I was so immersed in the culture. Well, two major things happened. First, I was brought up by entrepreneurs and I couldn't stop thinking about business. I felt like there was something else I should be doing. Second, after spending 30 days touring in a van with 7 guys, I felt like the culture wasn't giving back. I was doing too much and not getting enough in return. That was, and still is, a valuable lesson — to keep the culture alive you have to ensure the culture continues to be as rewarding as it was creating it. If you constantly make it a rewarding experience, the culture will continue to reward its host, the company.

So how do you create that culture? Well, first of all, you can't create a culture that feels contrived. Do you enjoy feeling like herded sheep? Nobody else does, either. Creating a culture needs to be an organic experience. You can't suddenly pronounce, "OK, we are now going to think about Digital Transformation." If you do that, a lot of smirks and rolling eyes will follow. Start by taking your managers aside and asking them directly, "How do you think we can digitally transform this company?" Then ask their reports, and then their reports. If you have a company of thousands get your managers to do it, but the more people the CEO talks to, the more people will talk about it. Once everyone is talking about it, then you can start discussing it en masse. If you do it this way, everyone feels they were part of the birth of the idea and you have now created a Digital Transformation Culture! Remember, culture is ignited from on high, but it's set ablaze by the whole.

### MAKE IT A CROWDSOURCED CONTEST

People use crowdsourcing for all kinds of different things. It is no longer a novel idea; today, it is an effective tool. We talked about creating a position and a culture within your company, but everybody loves a shot at being a winner. Hold on ... don't shake your head about how a crappy contest is not going to get results. First, this isn't a crappy small-time contest because it's going to have a great prize. Second, one smart employee is going to have face time with the CEO which could open up all kinds of possibilities for the employee. However, the big reason this works is it's going to allow that employee to be the smartest one in the room. If you don't think this last piece is a motivator then you haven't been in enough meetings or you are dominating them too much yourself, so pipe down and listen more. Smarty pants are everywhere.

The greatest ideas to transform a company can come from everywhere, and anywhere. Opening up the field to your entire staff will give you more to consider and it is going to make everyone feel involved. I use crowdsourcing when I can and I am a big fan of it for certain things like logo design. I have used *99designs* for a few logo designs and have been more than happy with the results. Typically, a designer gives you a few designs to look at, and you become tied to those for no better reason than that is all you saw. When you are dealing with 50 designers through crowdsourcing you see things you never imagined, and sometimes you'll be pleasantly surprised. P.S. That's a Digital Transformation in itself.

Sure, we're talking about bigger things than logo design but the bottom line is crowdsourcing works, and works quickly because, remember, it's a contest. Make sure you are not cheap with the prize and don't limit it to just your top managers. Crowdsource it blindly or get everyone into a giant group, either way you get to use the power of many brains instead of just one. This takes nothing more to start than figuring out the reward, so get this rolling ASAP! For all you know, Joe Smith may just be sitting in a cubicle with the idea to cut huge costs and absolutely ignite the growth of your business and all he is waiting for is the "put me in coach" moment. Take this and combine it with creating a real Digital position and culture and you now have a company that is warmed up and ready to transform.

# 13
## DIGITAL TRANSFORMATION TO
## KEEP EMPLOYEES

My dad was an extremely tough guy and an absolute force to be reckoned with. I don't mean that tongue in cheek. By the time he was 16 he had already owned 3 motorcycles and 2 cars. By the time he was 17, he was stabbed in a greaser fight (yep, he was a greaser like the movie Grease but not quite the dancer John Travolta was). By the time he was 19 he was working two jobs, married, and had a kid on the way. By the time the baby came he was fired, and by the time I was born, the guys that fired him were coming to him for a job. He was a rough and tough businessman and, to be honest, you wouldn't want to be in business against him — or with him. My mom was the brains of the operation and she was a deeply moral and ethical person, so needless to say, their marriage wasn't meant to last — but they were a good business team.

The old man was extremely judgmental and when it came to doing business he had a few rules. One that really stuck with me was his fascination with shoes. I don't mean a Paris Hilton fascination—he'd discriminate based on their look and quality. I had heard that people look at your shoes when they first meet you, but my dad's lack of political correctness really drove it home. When I was playing music, he would surprise me and show up at some of my gigs. He would walk in with his usual swagger, and with some new girl under his arm. When we played music we were always professional and always, always, wore suits. I remember the first time he came to one of my gigs I was really proud I was wearing a suit (even though it was not quite tailored) as I sat down with him. He looked me up and down and said, "That suit looks like shit. You need to go out and get a new suit. You also need to get a new pair of shoes because those look like shit too." I told him, "Dad I don't have the money for a new suit." He then looked at me very seriously and said, "Dom, let me tell you something that I don't want you to ever forget ... Nobody, and I mean nobody, wants to do business with a loser, so looking like a loser is not an option. Figure it out." If you think about that and get past the rough delivery, that is extremely profound. He was right, nobody wants to do business with a loser and sometimes, a business can look like a loser. Even successful businesses limit their full potential because they look like digital losers.

A company can look like a loser both outside and inside. Have you ever worked in or walked into an office where the place felt dead? That made you feel like you wanted to run away? Did you start running? There are lots of reasons why people want to leave their jobs, but if you look at any list of "Ten Reasons Why Companies Lose Top Talent", they all say in one version or another that top talent leave because they are not excited by the company vision.

Your top talent at any one time is usually your 40-54 year olds. These people are at an age when they feel they are in the know. They are fortunate enough to have one foot in traditional business and another in digital. These are the go-getters who not only want a digital vision, they expect one. Because, these people are Gen Xers and they have colleagues like me who preach smashing it on the web every day. If it isn't your competition that is waking them up to the fact your business model is the equivalent of a freaking 8-track player, it's their perception of a huge opportunity being squandered and eventually their careers. It's the leader's job to identify talent, passion and energy and, once identified, actually do something with it. If you don't, these rock stars are going to go somewhere else and take all that energy, experience and passion with them.

Even if the issue is not vision and excitement, maybe the lack of Digital Transformation makes everyone's job difficult and frustrating.

Are your employees still sending out faxes? Are they still receiving paper faxes on a fax machine? If they are, you are a digital basket case. I haven't received a paper fax in at least 7 years. Paper shuffling wastes time, money — and passion.

In fact, total paper consumption in North America was reduced by 24% from 2006 to 2009 as per the RISI World Pulp Annual Historical Data. That is pretty impressive. I'm sure the trend to decrease paper consumption will continue and that is a sign of digitization. Get with the trend.

You might ask yourself what does this have to do with control? Paper pushing means you're not digital, and consequently, you're wasting time having your employees wrestle with serious inefficiencies. What if you could reduce your employees' everyday tasks by 10%? Imagine every process in your company that does the paper shuffle is gone. That is just one baby step of Digital Transformation and the difference it can make. There are hundreds more to be embraced that will make your company more efficient, and make your employees a lot happier.

My friend, Richard Reid, is a gregarious and highly intelligent guy who runs a very innovative private equity fund. He has weeded through hundreds of businesses and with that experience comes an awful lot of knowledge. One morning we were walking and talking and he challenged me with this question:

Richard: Dom, do you know what the most important asset of a business is?

I started rattling off all the typical stuff.

Richard: Yeah, that's all good but it's nothing without energy! Because without energy a business is nothing but a husk, and it may last for a while, but not for long."

Richard is absolutely right and you can't afford to waste that energy. When your employees are unhappy about your lack of digital vision or all of the broken systems they have to work with, or all of the paper shuffling, they get disillusioned, complacent and lazy, and they lose interest. That is an energy killer.

If you have passionate energetic ass-kickers that need to channel their energy and great ideas, you must feed the need. If you force your employees to work in a static model that will lead to the company's long-term death, you are going to lose top talent. If you have a vision that inspires everyone, you are going to get the most productivity possible from your employees. They are going to be excited, and I promise they will be coming to you with either cost savings or revenue-generating ideas.

I have yet to see a company where the staff wasn't excited about a Digital Transformation. It's new, it's fresh, it's the right thing to do, and they feel like they are part of something groundbreaking—because they are.

## CRM — Stop being scared

One of the easiest ways to make things simple for your employees is to use CRM (Customer Relationship Management) software! Do you have any idea how many companies that bring in millions of dollars still don't have CRM? It's possibly one of the easiest ways to help increase sales and marketing, manage customers and leads, and relieve a ton of internal employee pain. If you're not using it, implement it now. I understand — when I first heard about CRM I was frightened because I had no idea what it meant. Of course, that was about 12 years ago, but now everyone knows about CRM. What has really changed is now there are a number of cloud based CRM solutions that are incredibly low cost.

Maybe you think you have such a unique business that no off-the-shelf CRM software will work for you. Maybe you're right, but understand there are thousands of programmers waiting to customize it for you and, since there are thousands, it's a buyer's market.

Salesforce.com is one of the big ones, and a pretty good system. However, I have used a few simple, less expensive ones like Zoho.com that are great and seamlessly integrate into marketing email systems. I have also been part of a complete Sugar CRM customization and I can tell you that anything is possible. From taking in orders or documentation off the web, to putting through the orders, to tracking fulfillment and shipping, to invoicing, to sending feedback forms after the fact, to marketing to the entire database, it's all there and it's all in the cloud. I suggest using a cloud-based CRM as you are going backwards if you don't.

If you do have CRM, make sure you are using it to the fullest. CRM without an integrated marketing campaign is just a fancy

Rolodex. When you have good CRM and embrace all of its potential, you have a mighty marketing force that extracts all the juice out of the squeeze.

If you don't have CRM, go for it right now! Put down the book, and either you or someone in your organization assess a few CRM systems, then make your decision, sign up, and get rolling. You will thank me, and in the end, your staff and customers will thank you, I promise.

# 14
# OWN YOUR CUSTOMERS

A t an early age I learned a powerful lesson without realizing it —
you must own your customers.

I started going to nightclubs when I was 14. Yeah I know that
sounds young, but we didn't have anything else to do. I would use my
buddy Andreas's older brother's I.D. to say I was 18. That allowed
me to go to 18-and-older clubs in the USA and then all the clubs in
Tijuana, Mexico, which was the ultimate destination for kids in San
Diego during the 80's. Realistically, you could have showed up with
a library card with the name, IAM UNDERAGE, and the Mexican
bouncers would have let you in. By the time I was actually 18 we all
had fake ID's saying we were 21 and we were going to real clubs. It
was a crazy time and little did I know I would experience a significant
lesson that I keep in mind for every business I touch.

Back then, a trend started to emerge. A wave of club promoters
started to offer something to clubs and restaurants they really needed:
customers. Lots and lots of customers. These guys had mailing lists a
mile long. The tactics were simple; they would send out, and when I
say "send out," I mean letters in the mail, inviting you to a "promoted
night". If you got one of these invites, you cancelled everything
because you knew it was going to be a really fun night, and the place
would be packed. They had perfect demographics—about a 50/50
girl-to-guy ratio.

They commanded such a huge audience that they could take a
struggling old run-down restaurant, clear the place out, bring in a DJ,

and their huge crowd would drink the place dry. It was brilliant and when a location wasn't giving the promoters what they needed, or got greedy on the split of the door and alcohol, BOOM, the promoters would move the entire club to another location. They had all the power because THEY OWNED THE CUSTOMERS!

If you take this story and substitute manufacturers for clubs and distributors for promoters, you see the biggest problem manufacturing faces: they don't own their customers.

My philosophy is always own your customers. In the past this may have been difficult but now we can digitally transform any business to do just that. The problem is businesses that work through distributors have their heads in the sand as far as who actually owns the customers. I find this willful ignorance most often in manufacturers. I was asked recently in an interview what I thought the biggest blind spot in manufacturing was and I gave a simple answer: denial. Denial about who actually owns the customer.

This isn't just a manufacturing issue, but a broader issue for all businesses. Nonetheless, the best way to illustrate this is through a recent interview I had entitled "Quit Relying on Distributors" by Mark Borokowski for Canadian Business Journal's July 2014 edition about manufacturing and branding. I've inserted this because I don't feel I can say it any clearer. The full interview can be viewed at CBJ.ca.

**MB: Dominic, you deal with all kinds of different industries and businesses but what are the real blind spots out there right now when it comes to manufacturing and distribution?**

*They seem to change day to day but the blind spot that is most glaring lately is plain old denial. People hire me to bring about change, and to do that I need to be a denial killer. I always bring that to my own businesses, my clients, and when I speak publically. So in that spirit...the days of owning a business and putting it on auto-pilot to churn out money for 30 years, are gone. The days of a business being handed down from generation to generation and surviving under the same business model, are gone. And the days of letting distributors own your end customers, are gone...however, most businesses and especially manufacturers still don't want to face this, hence all the denial.*

**MB: Definitely some tough realities but are you saying that manufacturers should break their distributor relationships?**

*Absolutely not, but what I am saying is that manufacturers need to form a relationship that most of them don't have, an end-customer relationship. Distributors are a necessary evil that block the end-customer relationship and they are in the "sell as much stuff as we can for the highest margins" business so the day you can't provide that anymore, your relationship with them is over. As soon as you become undesirable either through your pricing, products, delivery, or anything else a new competitor can provide that you can't, you're gone. If you are sitting there thinking there is no way your distributors would do that to you, or you have rock solid agreements that won't allow it, then what about the new distributor that pops up and crushes your "loyal" distributor and leaves you out in the cold? This is the reality today and it's war, but those that have armed themselves with great weapons have a great shot at winning.*

**MB: What are the weapons?**

*Smash everything you know and create a platform that lets you actually own your customers and emblazon your brand in their brains. The easiest way to do this is through an aggressive and comprehensive digital strategy. I am not just talking about a website. I am talking about a way to bring in tons of customers into the brand, get them into the culture, get a hook into them and make them loyal. Give them tools, make it easy to do business with you, and for God's sake actually sell them something.*

*I can hear your excitement about this but give me an example.*

Sure. Let's say you're a shoe manufacturer and you sell your shoes only through distributors because you are in fear of angering them if you sold direct. These distributors sell your shoes and about 100 others, and they constantly grind you on price. Then you decide to get smart and digitally transform your business. You create a strong brand and a website that is more than just a static brochure. You create an incredible front door that makes it exciting to walk through. When your customers arrive to the site there are a lot of things for them to be able to interact with, thereby interacting with your company. I call this "Dynamic Interaction" and it's part of my 4 pillars of Digital Transformation. Your customers are now excited enough to actually do something, and lo and behold, they spend time on the site interacting, but the real centerpiece is that they can buy a pair of shoes. This is just the first step because now you own this customer and you can market to them and sell them more things and it also allows them to bring more people into your world, not your distributors. In addition to this, digital marketing is kicking in to bring new customers to your site and once they have arrived, we use tactical strategies to follow people around the web for the next 500 days to continue to get your brand in front of them. YOU FINALLY OWN THE CUSTOMER!

*MB: This is a 2 part question. 1. I know it is happening but it's hard to believe that following someone around the web is actually allowed. 2. Aren't distributors going to get pretty cranky about you selling online?*

You'd think it would be illegal but it's not and Google is one of the main providers of this platform that is being used every day. We do this for all kinds of clients and I have done this for my own businesses, and have had great results. In fact, for certain industries that have competitors with strong Facebook followings, we can actually target your competitor's followers and place ads in front of them. It's the Wild West out there and it's good to be Wyatt Earp.

Distributors aren't going to get cranky if you structure the deal right. In fact, imagine someone comes to your site and the functionality of the site tells them "you are 10 minutes away from a location that has the shoes you want." This is completely easy to do and it will help push business to the stores, but now you own these customers and they are going to the stores with your shoes in mind. In addition, there are other ways to structure this to bring the distributor in on the sale but you're in the driver's seat because you own the customer. I don't care if you are selling something like fasteners, a relationship can be built and your brand can be built into a juggernaut.

**MB: So this isn't just a switch to marketing, it's actually a switch of the model itself.**

Exactly. People are waiting for you to tell them what to do. This is what makes Apple so successful. I have owned Apple products and I am not a fan, but what I am a fan of is their marketing because they create experiences, not products. They have actually been able to make you feel like you're 17 and there is a party going on, and if you don't buy their products you're the loser at home watching reruns of the Love Boat. In my eyes, Apple is a marketing company that happens to make products. Not the other way around.

It all starts with having a fantastic brand that people can relate to, and brands can be built. Some people might think that they have a boring product and there is no way to brand it. I say that is absolute B.S. because who would have thought you could brand duct tape or glue? I can't help but buy Gorilla Glue or Gorilla Duct Tape when I have a choice. That's good branding, and

*I promise that there isn't a company out there that can't be branded to smash their industry.*

*However, this shouldn't be viewed as a science experiment. It's a giant artistic white board session and there's nothing more exciting than taking a company that has been stuck in a model and transforming them into what I like to call, Customer Acquisition Engines. It just brings the energy of the company and its employees up about 100 notches, leading to a surge of revenue growth. There is almost nothing more exciting to watch, and for manufacturing companies this is imperative because it allows them to quit relying on distributors and own their customers!*

In conclusion, we need to own our customers and when we digitally transform, we need to do it to own our customers. Whether that is going direct to them via digital or making your product somehow digital, you need to get to your end customer and own them. Some of the lowest hanging fruit can be found by working your brand digitally to generate more direct sales. Go from being a manufacturing company to a brand that manufactures. When you continually evolve your business digitally, your brand evolves with it, making it more important than anything else. Now you are the club promoter who says where the party is going to be, because you own the customers! Next, we are going to learn how to go and get them.

# 15
# DIGITAL MARKETING FOR DOMINATION

Digital marketing is a component of an overall digital strategy and this book wouldn't be complete unless we delved into it just a little bit. It's widely misunderstood and one of the things people ask me about the most. It's like crack cocaine for those that don't know what they're doing – it'll drain your bank account and leave you wanting. It's like driving a car for those that know what they're doing – learn how, get started, follow the rules, and, over time, become a good driver. Either way, everyone is excited about it but it remains a huge mystery to most businesses — even though it is much easier to understand than a full Digital Transformation. A few ground rules: forget everything you think you know about digital marketing and read with your Wonder Theory engaged.

Too many people crash and burn in their first foray into digital marketing because they do it all wrong. Most of the time it's a variation of putting up an ad on Google Adwords — they write it, choose a few keywords, fund the account with a credit card, and away they go. That can be done in about 20 minutes, and after Google reviews the ad it is likely to be online in hours. Bang, Bang, Bang. I like to call these people the premature marketers of digital marketing. They go into it too fast and blow their budget too quickly and end up feeling like it didn't work. The point is digital marketing works brilliantly, but only when you go into it with a strategy and are knowledgeable about the process.

The same thing with blogs. I touched on blogs earlier in this book, but this is another aspect of digital marketing that is often executed incorrectly, over and over. All the people telling you what a great idea it is to have a blog usually leave out the part about having to consistently come up with great content. That's the hard part — and the number one reason there's a graveyard of millions of blogs that were started with an article or two, and then put out to pasture. Blogging takes time and is an absolute pain in the butt if you are trying to do it all by yourself.

So, when it comes to a company being digitally savvy in this overly busy world with not enough employees, it's important to find out how you can interact with current customers and all of your potential customers without needing more staff. This is what the true miracle of digital marketing is all about.

Before I take you down the current digital marketing road, let's take a look at how people used to do it.

## THE EARLY YEARS — NOT DIGITAL

Here is how companies in the 20th century found new customers:

- Had a sales force cold calling
- Went to networking events and trade shows
- Asked for referrals
- Advertised in newspapers, TV, magazines, outdoor & radio
- Direct mail
- Sent out catalogues
- Knocked on doors
- Joined clubs

## THE EARLY DIGITAL YEARS

Here is how companies found customers from 2003 up until about 2 years ago:

- Google Adwords
- Wrote blogs to attract customers

- Emailed market through blast mails, bought lists
- Paid for banners on specific sites
- Online affiliate programs
- Tried to place articles on article sites
- SEO back-linked campaigns
- Spam, Spam, Spam

During the first 10 years of the new millennium it was all about traffic. The shotgun approach that said, "Get traffic to your site and hopefully someone will buy." But there was no plan anticipating what kind of traffic was coming to the site or what to do when people got there.

In contrast, blogs were, and still are, very good at getting the right kind of traffic to your site — as well as helping establish both your company and brand. One reason millions of blogs fell by the wayside is because companies didn't know how to properly gain traction from their blogging activity because the blogs were not properly directing traffic to a conversion event. *A conversion event is when a customer visits your site and you convert them into a process that is either an immediate or eventual sale.*

There are two main reasons people abandoned their blogging activities: it was too much work, and/or it wasn't creating sales. It takes a while to start generating traffic and business through great content. Some things listed above were much faster-acting than blogs, but as you will see there are a lot of new, different ways to get traffic, and those ways are constantly changing.

## NOW AND THE FUTURE

Now: The smart people got smarter. Here is how companies that are advanced in digital marketing have been driving traffic to convert into sales for the past couple of years.

- Surgical display network
- Surgical LinkedIn & Facebook placements
- Facebook email upload targeting

- YouTube
- Site retargeting
- Search retargeting
- Mobile
- Social Media through both organic postings and advertising campaigns
- Automated targeted email sequences

If you are looking at the list above and asking yourself, "what the heck is that stuff?" then you probably have just identified one area where you need a Digital Transformation — the area of digital marketing and all of the fantastic opportunities it brings. In fact, this is how your competitors might be killing you right now, and most definitely will be how new competitors will take away market share in the future. These are the tools of a whole new generation of businesses that understand the systems and understand the huge benefits that come along with it when it's done right. All of the things listed above are amazing at capturing new customers or helping nurture existing customers, if you know what you are doing. Either way, it drives revenue! If you don't know what you are doing, it will drive you into the ground.

I can hear the doubters. "I already have Google Adwords and it doesn't really work for me so how do I know any of this other digital drib drab is going to work?" Let me answer that question with a story.

The first time I ever played golf was on a business outing for Bell, and I remember my sales director using the word "tragic" when he watched me swing the club. After setting a new course record for lost balls, I went home that day with a very sore everything. I couldn't understand why it was so difficult to hit the ball well. I was able to get golf clubs, I was able to get on the course, I was able to have lots of shiny new golf balls, I wore very funny looking shoes, and if I was capable of being in control of all of those things, then why couldn't I golf like everyone else?

Answer: I didn't know how to swing the club. Any golfer in the world will tell you the key to golf isn't the equipment but instead, how you swing the club. How do you learn to swing the club? You may do a combination of a lot of things. You might hire a pro, practice on the driving range, read up on it, or watch videos on YouTube. A lot of work — no wonder the sport is on a decline in our instant gratification society.

Digital Marketing is no different because it takes an expert to know how to properly create and deploy a digital marketing strategy that is in line with the overall digital strategy and continue to optimize it. I call this Digital Engine Optimization (DEO). Anyone is capable of opening up a Google Adwords account, filling it up with money, writing an ad, and getting zero results. Which is like swinging a golf club, and watching it shank right or left while everyone else laughs their asses off.

How does everyone else digitally market so well? First, maybe only 2% do it well and that's because they know what they are doing or they hired a pro, or practiced writing ads, read books, and watched videos. Are you seeing the connection here to my tragic golf story? You can't land on the digital links for the first time and hit a hole in one. Just like golf, you have to keep on top of all of this because the advertising engines out there are living things that change all the time. That is why DEO is so important — it keeps the prospects coming by continually optimizing, and when you do that — the cash register rings.

At this point, let's engage our Wonder Theory and open our minds to look at this differently. I know this can be overwhelming so let's forget about all of the techniques and the stress, and look at this conceptually. Digital Marketing done well is the perfect combination of art and science. Let's look at both aspects.

## THE ART

Selling something with a radio or TV commercial, on a bus or a billboard, is different from selling it on the web. There is no instant interaction using traditional advertising (except for QR codes and that didn't take off the way everyone thought it would). The web on the other hand is all about interaction. I, the digital advertiser, need you to look at my ad and get excited enough to click through, which will take you to a conversion and sales event that further engages you, converts you and makes my sale. (Sales cycles vary so this can happen immediately or over time.)

This is an art form. Companies spend millions on ad agencies that are supposed to tell them who their demographic is, and how to convert that demographic into customers. However, many ad agencies are in the dark when it comes to digital marketing because many of them don't respect that it is a completely different discipline. It's like saying all medicine is the same, and a dentist can be a neurosurgeon and vice versa. The agencies that don't get it usually hire a kid out of college, call them a digital strategist, and throw a lot of client money down a rabbit hole.

The other part of the art is the constant need for new material. When you advertise on LinkedIn or Facebook you are going to blow through your demographic very quickly if you target properly. You need to come up with fresh material because your viewers constantly suffer from ad fatigue. Same thing for banner advertising and text ads. A good campaign will test and run multiple ads to find which ones perform best. This takes creativity.

Understanding where to find an audience is a bit of an art, as well. Sometimes places like Google and Facebook can't target as surgically as we need them to and we need to get creative. One company that I partnered with has a target market of commercial property owners that are selling their real estate. They found it very difficult to reach this market until we attacked the issue from a creative business angle. That is art. Not science.

You're probably thinking that you know there are ways to initiate massive growth through digital but it is too damn difficult to understand and execute. Don't worry about it, all you need to know is that it is possible. Your job is to put the people in place that do know what they are doing to plan (art) and execute (science). They will provide the creative digital tactics to drive your business forward, adjusting in response to your market — daily, hourly, by the minute.

Now, let's talk about the science.

## THE SCIENCE

Because we are talking about something that is running on the web, there is always science behind it. For example, lots of people know AdWords uses a bidding system, but what they don't know is that there's a massive algorithm that affects bids on Google's ad network. Any fool can spend thousands on an advertising budget and lose it all because they don't understand the algorithm. It's complex and it's a moving target but if you know what you're doing Google will reward you with showing your ads more while also charging you less. However, many amateurs don't even know how it works so they end up spending two to five times more on ads than they should. Digital advertising is all about numbers and you can bankrupt yourself on $5 per click advertising. The reason nerds all over the world offer AdWords Management is because there is an actual science to the process. These folks are digital scientists. Not beaker-and-burner science — digital science.

Did you know: in the virtual cloud there are massive ad servers that are ad exchanges, somewhat like the New York Stock Exchange? Some people buy, some people sell. The buyers want to place advertising. The sellers have web space to sell. That web space comes in all kinds of different formats that subscribe to the network, and offer space for ads on a web page like The Wall Street Journal, or your Aunt Connie's blog about knitting, or your teenager's free mobile app that forces them to look at advertising when they use it. Every millisecond, a ton of buys and sells happen. This is what is happening behind the scenes of Real Time Bidding (RTB). Good digital marketing managers know all about it, and utilize it to its maximum by placing ads at lower costs that are better targeted.

It's like managing a hedge fund but, instead, it's digital marketing. Can you imagine trying to mount and run your own hedge fund trading platform in one day? Well, that is basically what you are trying to do when it comes to setting up and launching your Adwords and digital marketing campaigns in a day. This is not an amateur's game and, just like the stock market, you can lose money fast if you don't know what you are doing, and you can make money if you have a disciplined platform. That, my friends, is the science.

I hope it's easy to see now that there is an art and a science to web marketing, and it's the combination of the two that make the design and execution of a digital marketing strategy work. If you think it's a heck of a learning curve to be able to do all of this yourself, you're right. That is why there is an entire industry built around this with people and platforms like HubSpot and Infusionsoft to make it easier. Get smart or get a nerd; either way you win.

## THE FUTURE

We know what you should be doing today, but let's have a little fun and peer into the future and see what all of this is going to look like in the next two years:

- GEO derived placement *aka* Big Brother is watching
  - Advertisers know exactly where you have been in the last two weeks. For example:
    - You visited a sport stadium in the last week, and you're targeted for advertising for different sporting events.
    - You went to a restaurant in the last week, and they hit you with restaurant advertising.
  - Screen Pops – You walk past a store in the mall and the store hits you with advertising or a coupon via your cell phone to entice you to come into the store.
- Gamification – turn a portion of your model or advertising into a game
- Mobile ads on apps target you with more precision
- Strong SMS push advertising to your phone
- Influencer Identification & Blast
- Bigger push on Real Time Bidding (RTB)
- Leadership Casting
- LMS Systems: Selling through learning

Wow, what a difference two years can make in the digital space!

I am being conservative when I say two years because a lot of this is already happening. THE WEB DIGITALLY TRANSFORMS

FASTER THAN YOU CAN. I put that in caps so you will wake up to the fact that if you haven't already digitally transformed, you need to, because someone else is going to do it — and you lose. Digital Marketing is a good example of how fast transformation can happen and that it will continue to evolve at blinding speed.

If you look at everything in the future list, one common theme is *Dynamic Interaction*. Digital Marketing is about interaction with your customers, and potential customers, and Digital Transformation is all about creating this interaction. Even in as simple a form as PPC, when your customers click on an ad (interaction) that takes them to a landing page (interaction), that in turn offers one or more options to engage (interact) with your company, you have created dynamic interaction. You offer an online sale, the downloading of digital material, a game, a subscription to a newsletter or a blog, as long as your visitors can interact with you. And that will turn your mundane web presence into a customer- acquisition engine.

Think about the example in Jimmy's Carpet business. That is about the dynamic interaction of customers with an app, of a carpet warehouse with the scheduling of the workforce and the confirmation of the client's availability. It is all *Dynamic Interaction*. These interactions are what lead to engaging a customer in an overstimulated world where you have one shot to win, and seconds to do it. Yes, folks, seconds.

When I digitally transformed the funeral business I had one mission and one mission only: own as many customers as I could. The only way to do that in that stodgy industry, without any of the infrastructure that my competitors had, was to offer Dynamic Interaction. Digitally market, allow clients to build a quote in front of their eyes, allow them to real-time chat with funeral directors, and follow up with email sequences. Enable them to receive all of their paperwork online, and follow up with online automated feedback forms. This was Dynamic Interaction in one of the most static industries on earth.

If I could do it for the funeral industry, I promise you it can be done for your company or industry, The identification of the enablement of Dynamic Interaction is your launching point for

Digital Transformation and all the tactics that are part of it like digital marketing.

## LEADERSHIP CASTING — A FUTURE TACTIC

Getting the word out about your business sometimes starts with broadcasting your voice. What if you could have a news team following you around catching all of the great things you have to say? What if they could then take all of those great thoughts you create as an industry leader and turn it into powerful content? Welcome to Leadership Casting. Leadership Casting is like blogging on steroids — but someone else does all the work. They extract all of your expertise and digitally broadcast it to the world to profile your leadership in your industry. Leadership Casting is the only thing I recommend that comes close to resembling SEO, and one of the few things in the organic SEO arena that works.

Leadership Casting is a disciplined integrated program for pushing out your message. It is one of the most powerful means to do so today. Imagine you had your own personal writer on staff that hardwired into your brain, and took all of those good ideas and crafted them into educational articles. Then that is blasted out to the web. Articles like those are just another way to dynamically interact with your customer base — but what is truly brilliant is it answers questions your customers have on a daily basis. This establishes you as the expert and builds virtual loyalty because you were able to answer their question with an article. As CEO's we hardly have time to answer the phone, so spending time blasting out our thoughts and ideas is out of the question.

Leadership Casting usually takes about two hours initially with you and then maybe 20 minutes a month thereafter, and then your voice begins to blast through the web in the form of articles. Imagine an article derived from your thoughts coming out every single week. Imagine it getting blasted out to LinkedIn, Facebook, article submissions, etc... Leadership Casting is web PR in a box and gives you all of the benefit without the heavy lifting.

The next chapter will tell you all about why I think SEO is dead with a few exceptions.

## SEO is Dead

Some of you may have noticed that I haven't mentioned Search Engine Optimization (SEO). I'm not going to spend a ton of time on this, but in my opinion SEO is dead. I expect people will write and tell me I don't know what I'm talking about, but I expect most of them will be SEO professionals and not business people. Businesses need long term strategies that create ROI and can't be shut off like a light switch by outside forces. SEO is no longer a strategy that has any longevity. How can I say that? Let me take you back a couple of years to when I created one of the most aggressive SEO campaigns on the planet.

SEO experts who saw what I designed, told me, "I have never seen anything like that before. You're crazy." In fact, Google would have come down to our office guns a-blazing and gone postal on us if they knew what we did. The execution was incredibly complex, but in essence the strategy was simple. People search for things in a way that are somewhat common sense. For example: If I am looking for a plumber in Chicago I will type in Chicago Plumber. If I was in Toronto, I would search Toronto Plumber or Toronto Plumbing Services or — something like that. Way back then, Google's algorithm gave heavy weighting to exact matched domain names, and pushed them up to the first page with just a little bit of SEO. So, if I wanted to take over plumbing, I would buy Chicagoplumbing. com. I went on a buying spree and bought tons and tons of domain names. I mean literally thousands. Then, we had a complex multi-domain content management system run almost 1,000 websites on every one of those individual domain names. Forget about redirecting domains to a single site, these were all individual, and unique enough to fool Google. We were killing it with this strategy and we were number one in almost all the searches. However, that all changed, on or about April 25, 2012.

Leading up to that date, Google had two major headaches. The first problem was the US Federal Trade Commission was threatening Google with a claim that Google was treating its competitors unfairly. In turn, they wanted Google to disclose their algorithm. Giving up their secret sauce was not an option. The second issue was SEO gurus were gaming Google's search engine to put their clients on the highly coveted page 1, position 1, spot.

On or around April 25th, depending on where you were in the world, Google dropped a massive nuclear bomb called Penguin, and they changed the algorithm. Digital death, panic, destruction and confusion followed. Sites that held the top ranked position for years found themselves on page 100 — if at all. What did show up on page 1, position 1, were sites like Yellow Pages, Super Pages, etc. that were directory sites. Let's be real, if people wanted to go to directory sites they would have gone to them before going to Google. Everyone started getting results from Google that weren't the most relevant, and all of the sites that were ever so gung-ho about SEO found years of time and money vaporized and they were back at the starting line.

We had an inkling this was coming, and shifted our strategy two months beforehand, but it took us time to get the new strategy humming.

Even though I was negatively affected by this, in my opinion what Google did was brilliant because of what they accomplished in a single stroke. The US Government dropped its case against Google — check off one big problem. Next, right around the same time, ads on Google looked less like ads, and the opaque advertising space on Google became more transparent, making the ads appear to be more like organic search results.

And what was the result? Businesses were shocked and awed after watching a ton of money they spent on SEO go down the drain.

In fact, an avalanche of businesses started to call it quits on SEO. Guess where all of that SEO money went? Google Ads. It was a bitter pill to swallow and it took a little while for many SEO stalwarts to surrender and say, "OK, let's buy ads, because we can at least count on the fact Google won't freeze us out tomorrow — that's how Google makes money." Google's ad revenues have always grown, but I'm convinced the rate would have been much slower if it hadn't been for the algorithm change. Slightly diabolical? Maybe, but at least acknowledge the brilliance.

I am not saying ranking well is impossible. If you work tremendously hard making your site relevant, and you have consistent unique and great content on your site that everybody wants to see, it can eventually happen. What I am saying is, if you rely on SEO tactics as the mainstay of your digital marketing strategy, Google will break your heart, and your business, by changing the algorithm again. This is not a "maybe", but a "when".

As I mentioned, great content surrounding general Leadership Casting of your company and its leaders is always a good strategy. If you have unique content that helps answer questions potential customers may have, or gives them information they need that they haven't even thought about yet, this can make those individual pages rank well. Especially if it is getting pushed around the social media channels. Call it great content, call it smart promotion, or call it SEO if you need to, but this is your best bet for ranking well organically.

Your main goal should always be to create a digital marketing model that you can count on long-term to drive new business consistently to your site. Digital advertising gives returns on a consistent basis because you pay people for that advertising space. They want your money, so they continue to give you the product. You need to optimize your digital advertising to make sure the Cost per Acquisition (CPA) makes sense. Once you do that, you have a platform for a customer acquisition engine that has longevity. Traditional SEO doesn't provide that because, at the end of the day, Google is just two guys with a website and they can do whatever the heck they want.

To close off, I want to give you a very simple and easy to understand flow of a basic digital marketing campaign while reinforcing the basic principles of sales. I call this, The Draw, The Comfort, and The Close.

## THE DRAW, THE COMFORT, AND THE CLOSE

Growing up, and to this day, one of my best friends is a guy named Andreas. Yep, the same Andreas I sold strawberries with. I met Andreas in the middle of the night when I was 13. He was walking down the street with Sam, who became one of my best friends as well. They had just been kicked out of a Catholic High School dance for trying to dance and pick up all of the girls. The problem was they weren't students at that high school, and the faculty and boys from the school weren't impressed with the interlopers that looked like they walked out of a Duran Duran video. Andreas was Greek and I was Italian and, culturally, we were an anomaly back then in San Diego. So, we became instant friends with our European similarities and dysfunctional families.

With a bunch of positive energy and a unique style, we unknowingly created an incredible marketing and sales technique to pick up girls. We would go to a club where we knew there were going to be a lot of girls. (The right audience.) Andreas is probably one of the most handsome guys you have ever seen. Girls literally flock to this guy and he didn't even have to say a thing. (The draw.) In fact, he hardly said a word as he played the strong silent type. Once the girls were glowing in the presence of Andreas, I would make them laugh and feel completely at ease. (The comfort.) And then, after the draw and the comfort, Sam would do his thing. Sam, oh Sam. He would somehow make the girls feel that we were more special than they were and they should be honored to be around us. (The close supported by value.) He was the master at making girls hate him, and then 20 minutes later, love him. We were an ultimate trifecta and it worked without us ever acknowledging it.

What we didn't realize was we were putting girls through the sales funnel. It all started with the Right Audience and then it was The Draw, The Comfort, and The Close.

Audience = The Right One

Draw = Marketing

Comfort = Right product/service on the right site with credibility

Close = The product/service has value and the audience wants it, creating a conversion event into a sale

Figure 4 will help you dip your pinky toe into digital marketing. There's an entire book's worth of information in this figure alone. Imagine this happening with your business on the web:

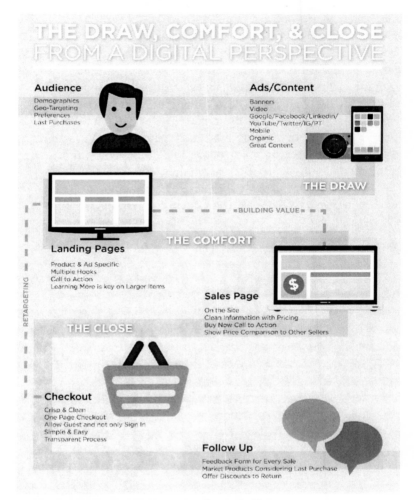

*Figure 4 – The Draw, Comfort, & Close*

Once that is built do you know how much time, effort, and money is needed to execute on a daily basis? Nada, Zip, Zero, Nothing! Except, however, for the digital marketing ad spend and the $10 – 30 a month in off-the-shelf software and spending a little money on outsourcing to keep it optimized.

This is called making money while you sleep, or what I like to call a sales force without the cost. Part of the initial build can be done with your in-house marketing and IT team, or you can hire someone to build it. Either way, we're not talking a lot of money. When it's all working I like to call this marketing phenomenon a Customer Acquisition Engine, and when you get it right, it becomes an engine that needs drops of gas instead of gallons. It goes and goes and goes. If the Audience doesn't buy right away, no problem, we keep retargeting them until they do. One day your mailing list has 5 people and your retargeting list has 20, and the next day you have 5,000 people on your mailing list and 20,000 on your retargeting list. It's the digital equivalent of perpetual motion.

Everything I am talking about is real, possible, and happening now. If you own a business you should be doing it. Put the book down and do it now!

# 16
## WEBSITE VS WEB STRATEGY

For about a year during my musician days I lived in a house that I rented with my Aunt Linda. I was 24, Aunt Linda was 34, and she partied like a freakin' rock star. One of the coolest things was that the house was right by the ocean in Pacific Beach, California. After I finished my daily practicing, I would head down to the beach around 5 pm for high tide, and I'd body surf before leaving to play that night.

Body surfing is one of the things I love most because it's probably the closest you can come to flying. Of course, if you don't know what you're doing, it is also the closest you'll ever come to being force fed sand and drowning.

The principal is simple, catch a wave right when it is about to start cresting, and let it take you. Then make like Superman flying, and go either right or left to stay inside the tube. If you try to catch the wave at the wrong place or at the wrong time, you either miss the wave, or get slammed into the ocean floor harder than Hulk Hogan dominating Wrestlemania.

Not catching the wave is the worst because you do a ton of paddling with no reward. Waves are biggest at high tide and usually come in sets with the bigger waves coming in sets of three. You have to be strategic waiting for the set, and then wait for the right wave in the set. There's nothing worse than catching a tiny wave, and missing all the big ones.

What is the recipe for being a great body surfer? In-shape body, great wave, good timing, and good strategy. Great body, no waves = failure. Great waves, out of shape body = failure. Great waves, great body, no strategy or timing = failure.

It's the same on the Web. **There is a world of difference between a website and a web strategy** *aka* **digital strategy.** A website is part of a web strategy.

I can assure you at least 90% of businesses that have a website, don't have a web strategy. They throw the site up, sit back, and wonder why they don't get any business from it. Well, it's easy to understand why it doesn't work, because it's like trying to body surf without the actual wave, timing or strategy. A website is only one component of your overall strategy. Think about what I'm saying here: a website without a strategy is like trying to body surf without a wave. Does that sound crazy? Does to me! However, I have sat with some absolutely brilliant business people, and they don't get it. Many times they feel that they have checked the box on a digital strategy because they just overpaid for a website. Sometimes, they are worn out from building the website, or they are too lazy, don't have the skill set, are overwhelmed, or don't see the opportunity. As far as excuses go, all of those are worse than what you told your parents when you came home at 5:00 a.m. as a teenager.

There are probably over 100 questions that we ask when it comes to the website alone, and if you haven't worked through the following in an exhaustive manner, you don't have enough to build a website, much less a digital strategy:

- The customer
    - Who are my customers?
    - Where are my customers?
- How much will my customers pay for my products? (Not how much you charge them, what will they pay?)
- Why are they coming to my site? To get questions answered? To learn? To buy?
- How can I dynamically interact with them?

- How will I convert them once I get them to my site?

    o How will I track and get them back if I haven't converted them?

- How much is my average sale?

- How much are we willing to spend on acquiring clients online *aka* Cost per Acquisition (CPA)?

- What is the average life cycle of a client, and how much will they spend over that lifetime?

- How will I sell them more things once they have bought from me?

- How will I market and sell them those additional products?

Forget about scratching the surface, this isn't even leaving a smudge from your pinky finger. These are just a few of the burning questions that need to be answered before you even think about creating a digital strategy, and then design, or redesign, a website. When I work with companies, and we go through this discovery process, people tell me they feel like they have given birth by the time we are through!

You know why? Because by going through this process we give birth to a beautiful baby named "Strategy" and, once she's born, she grows rapidly. Refer back to the Digital Strategy Diagram in Chapter 10, but now that you know so much more than you did at the beginning of the book, I am hoping you'll see this with educated eyes.

This is the beginning of the deep internet age we are into, and you can't have a static website with zero strategy and expect it to drive business. That might have worked once, because it was a very small crowd out there. But things have changed and you are going to drown if you try that now. You must understand there are several components to a digital strategy — and the website is just one.

## Does Digital Transformation Start with a Website?

In many cases yes, but not always. Maybe Digital Transformation for your company is about operations and the supply chain. Maybe it's an app that transforms how your customers interact with you. Maybe, in the beginning, using CRM is enough of a transformation as a start. Maybe it's transforming parts of your business that don't touch the end customer or suppliers.

However, remember the Four Pillars of Digital Transformation. Dynamic Interaction usually occurs on the web or app level. That dynamic interaction could be happening inside the company, and it could be your starting point to bring the customer into your world, expose them to your hooks and convert them into a customer.

**Your website is your front door to do that.** I cannot emphasize this enough. I am confident when I say it's more important than the front door of your office and, in fact, more people walk through your virtual door than your bricks-and-mortar one. Why would anyone want to walk in and do business with you, if your front door looks like an abandoned building with graffiti on its broken windows? Remember the immortal words of my father, "Nobody wants to do business with a loser." Make sure your website is absolutely AWESOME! Make it professional, beautiful, cool, credible and functional.

I am asked daily about my opinion on digital strategies for multiple businesses and, of course, the first place I look is their website. I can't help myself, but it's a fact — that's going to give me a really good indication of what I am walking into. Of course, the first question the CEO asks me is about their website and I have to be blatantly honest — it's great or it is a freakin' abomination. As a result, over the years I have formulated a very simple test (almost subconsciously). The funny thing is — you, me, and everyone else puts every website through this same test. I call this my 3-for-3 Rule as a starting point for any site to be successful.

The 3-for-3 Rule is all about what is happening **above the fold.** That's the space you see on a screen before scrolling. Yes, people do scroll, but we must motivate the visitor above the fold to get them to continue on.

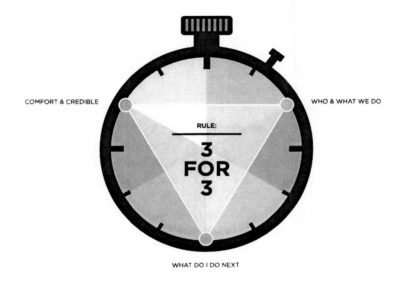

COMFORT & CREDIBLE

WHO & WHAT WE DO

RULE:

**3 FOR 3**

WHAT DO I DO NEXT

## *Figure 5 – 3 for 3 Rule*

The 3-for-3 Rule says a customer should experience 3 things in the first 3 seconds of showing up to your site:

1.  **Know Who and What You Are**

    "We are Domino's Pizza, and we serve Pizza, wings, and sandwiches." Funny enough, Domino's fails this test. Nowhere above the fold of their website does it say Domino's. Just the logo in the top left hand corner. Dear Domino's, there are a million pizza places out there and though we may have found you through search, and though we are a fan of your forward thinking for Digital Transformation, you need to start with your website because there's a whole generation that might not know you. Failed!

2.  **Comfort and Credibility/Authenticity**

    Your business is reputable as demonstrated through either media coverage or social media proof like testimonials and Facebook posts. You show experience and know-how.

119

I cannot tell you how many sites do this *wrong,* and they usually put the media coverage under the fold. Companies like Angie's List are massive and even they get it wrong. I might have heard about Angie's List from a friend but I have to scroll to the bottom of the homepage to find out that they have been featured on CBS, ABC, FOX, etc. As a visitor, I might not ever get there.

**3. What do I do next?**

Click Here to Get Started, Click Here to Learn More, Choose One, etc. Clean calls to action are critical. On propelactive. com we made sure to hit people with one call to action, Sign up Your Business! It's that simple. Instagram's home page has a crisp call to action – Download on the App Store or Get in on Google Play. In fact, it's the only thing you can do on their homepage, besides logging in to an already existing account. Simple.

Sometimes the 3-for-3 Rule can be bent a little, but only in unique situations. One of my clients has a client base of extremely wealthy individuals. Their company is extremely successful, but they knew they needed help with their overall image and digital strategy. We started with their front door — the website. Their website looked like they were a tiny shop out of a one-horse town in Nebraska. It utterly failed to communicate to the world the brilliance of the company and knowledge of the staff. In fact, we all agreed their current website was making them lose business.

How did we fix it? We turned the site into a platinum masterpiece. Now, when you arrive you know you're dealing with a global player. They can handle whatever you throw at them. You know they are professional, reliable and, most importantly, trustworthy. Now their site looks as exclusive as their clientele.

We actually broke a rule the way we built the website. Their clients are all extreme millionaires. We thought it was more important to wow them first, and then give them the calls to action and credibility. It is a strategy that has worked well, but only as an exception.

Your website must start to communicate the moment it loads. Every part of it — if you're a restaurant make me feel the type of food, the greatness of that food, the people that love the food, and the people that love to make it. If you are a doctor make me feel like I'm in your clinic, warm, safe and assured it is the kind of place that can help me. If you're a daycare center make me feel protected, educated — and let me feel the fun. Do you get the picture?

Remember — your website is only one component of your entire digital strategy, but it is the component that the world will judge you by. It is your starting point. However, do not even think about designing or redesigning your website until you have a digital strategy in place. Otherwise, you are going to redesign it again, a year from now, and over and over again. Lastly, in our world today sometimes an app is the front door. It too should respect the 3-for-3 Rule while trying to motivate someone to download. In fact, try using the 3-for-3 Rule as an opener of business conversations. You might just find that you save a lot of time and effort by getting to the point.

# 17

# THE BIGGEST EXCUSE FOR NOT TRANSFORMING - TIME

When I speak at seminars and conferences I am constantly impressed by the overwhelming interest in Digital Transformation. I see more and more business leaders who realize its importance, and I'm always excited to share their enthusiasm. But what happens after that? They are all fired up and they don't know how to follow up. They'll use all kinds of excuses to excuse and explain, but the one I hear most often is "time". No surprise, as that's the excuse we use for everything. I want you to understand how important it is not to let time be an excuse. To do so, I want to take you back to a world that always keeps time.

After making some headway playing music I started to get deeply into jazz. I don't mean elevator Muzak, I mean intense, blow-your-hair-back, late-Fifties, early-Sixties bebop jazz. It happened because of a fateful meeting on a San Diego street. I met a trumpet player named Gilbert Castellanos and we hit it off right away. He had just finished a tour of Europe opening for Wynton Marsalis. Gilbert was one hundred times the musician that I was. He said he was starting a group and I volunteered to introduce him to the more seasoned bass players in town. He looked at me and said, "I want you to play bass." I blinked and told him I wasn't good enough to play with him. He replied, "Don't worry about that. You're going to practice your ass off and you'll get good. You have fire and that is something you can't teach."

Well, I practiced my ass off 8 hours a day and then played a 4 hour gig almost every night. I played 12 hours of music a day and I was getting crushed every single night. Absolutely crushed. We had a great drummer and playing with him felt like trying to hold on to the back of a car bumper doing donuts.

As a jazz bass player you play quarter notes and you play a note every beat. This meant keeping time was my most important job. I learned that whatever was happening, cymbal crashes, crazy time signatures, anything, time moves with or without you. I got to the point where I could feel the perpetual nature of time because my fingers played every single quarter note and if I stopped, time would take off without me and I would be left behind. If I tried to go too fast, time kept going at its own pace and I would be out of sync. You can't control time and, whatever you do, you need to know it is going to happen, with or without you.

*Time lesson #1 — Time is going to keep moving no matter what — whether you play with it or against it. If you keep waiting to make a move, time will take off without you and so will your competition. Saying you don't have enough time to make a move is saying you don't have enough time to be an active successful business. The more time you waste waiting, the less time your business has to survive.*

I hate learning something the wrong way and as a musician part of my learning curve was to properly play stand-up bass. The stand-up bass is a very physical instrument if you don't know what you're doing. I didn't know what I was doing. I started taking lessons from all of the seasoned guys in town to help me with my technique. My two main teachers were Bob Magnusson, and Chris Conner, and they both had beautiful technique and had played with some of the greatest jazz musicians in history. After a while, they told me it was time for me to be classically trained because bass is an orchestral instrument, and the classical guys really had the best technique around. At the time, the San Diego Symphony was on strike for what seemed like a year, and the principal bassist, Jonathan Green, agreed to take me on as a student.

He completely tore down my technique. To the ground. I started to be concerned because it was seriously affecting my playing. Everything slowed down because I had to relearn how to play bass.

I didn't have time for relearning, because playing was how I made money. When I told him that, he explained that if I didn't take the time to fix my technique, the bass would eventually tear my hands apart, and I would be an arthritic mess. Do you see any business parallels here? The lesson was (and still is), I had to stop what I was doing, take the time to learn a new, better way of doing it, and if I did, I would be twice as good as I was before.

Time lesson #2 — *Taking the time to learn or try a new direction is sometimes the hardest thing to commit to. It feels like you're slowing your business down by doing it. Look beyond the decision, the planning and implementation, and focus on what your business will look like after you're done. You'll realize slowing down actually sped you up in the long run.*

My life back then was like an incredible dream. Every morning I woke up and went out to breakfast with the band. We would talk about the music, the girls from the night before, and eat *huevos rancheros*. Then I would go back home and practice for 8 hours. Start of the evening, I would shower, suit up, and go to the gig. Some nights we would go out afterwards, but the schedule would start over again the next day. It took four hard years of playing with Gilbert, studying my technique, and practicing daily to turn me into a professional jazz musician. It was an incredible life at the time.

One morning we went to one of our breakfast hangouts and we had a fateful meeting with the star, John Mueller, of the theatre production The Buddy Holly Story. John said the show was coming to town and could we help by connecting them with any stand-up bass players. It was a crazy coincidence but they had to urge me to audition because I was so stuck in my routine that I thought the two hours it would take to audition was going to mess with my daily practice time. *I also didn't want to waste the time to go after a new opportunity as I was happy doing what I was doing.*

Finally, I went — just to see if I could get the gig, as I had never auditioned for theatre before. I went to the audition, finished, walked out feeling like a big shot because, after jazz, Buddy Holly was easy. This lady chases me down and says, "Where are you going?" I said I just did the audition and I was done. She said, "That was the music audition, you still need to audition your acting parts in front of the director." Acting parts? What the hell are you are talking about lady? "I didn't know there were acting parts." She replied," Honey, this is Buddy Holly and the Crickets, and you are auditioning to be one of the Crickets." Well, that made me feel actually dizzy. They wanted me to act?

I then had the most awesome two minutes of my life auditioning with one of the craziest directors around, Sam Woodhouse of the San Diego Repertory Theatre. I was brought into a room and paired up with another "actor" that was trying out to be the drummer. I swear to God this is exactly what he said, "You are 19, you're from Lubbock, Texas, all you care about is music and pussy. GO!"

I guess I was able to channel that because they offered me the part but I was still hemming and hawing about taking it because I was worried about *the time it would take away from what I was doing*. Then Sam (the director) sat down with me and said something to me I will remember forever. He said, "Dominic, you can play music for the rest of your life, but you can act *right now*." Well, that woke me up like diving into an icy pool, and I ended up taking the part and it was one of the best decisions of my life. The show was a smash hit and I learned a ton and it made me a better musician overall. In fact, I think it actually made me a better person because it gave me a confidence I didn't have before, and it gave me the calmness that comes with it. Lucky for me I took the time to go after that new and unknown opportunity.

*Time lesson #3 – We always think there is never enough time for the business we already have, and taking the time to look at a new opportunity is impossible or unnecessary. However, you must constantly take the time to look at new opportunities because that is what may drive the business forward, and in fact, may become the business in the future.*

After Buddy Holly I went back to playing jazz and studying classical. Things in San Diego started feeling stagnant. I was *doing the same thing I always had done* and I didn't feel like I was growing as a musician, or a person. I almost began resenting everything I was doing and anybody associated with it. I felt like I needed a change.

Then John Mueller, who had played Buddy Holly, called. He said the show was going to Toronto and he asked if I would go. I grabbed that opportunity for everything it was worth. I jumped through a million hoops to make it happen and sold my car, got rid of my place, and got on a plane with my bass and my clothes. *I* knew it was time to make a change and my plan was not to come back for a while. Little did I know it would be forever.

*Time lesson #4 – Everything requires renewal and transformation. When your business model has become habitual, it's time to stop doing what you've always been doing and make a change, even a drastic one. It may be that decision not only reinvigorates your business, but it also reinvigorates you!*

Time and money are the oldest excuses around so don't be typical by using either one. Be a leader, be a trailblazer, be more than you or anyone else ever believed you could be. Take every minute, hour, day or week and make a choice to either use it, or let it be used against you. If you don't have money for certain initiatives, innovate. Run like you are being chased by the hounds of hell, because your competitors are coming, and if you do the right things, all they'll eat is your transformation dust!

# 18
## PLANT THE SEEDS

THE CYBER OCEAN—TRANSFORMATION IS WHAT AND HOW

The Blue Ocean Strategy was all the rage for a while. I really like the book because anyone who believes in innovation and not doing the same old, same old, has my respect. If you haven't read Blue Ocean Strategy, my primitive summary is: stop competing head-to-head with competition and go after new markets and new customers.

In my opinion the best way to do that is digital. Let's call it the Cyber Ocean Strategy. The foundation of this strategy is to digitally sell people things they could never buy before. You might say, "Dom, are you just talking about creating new products for people, because if you are, that is not profound." No, what I am saying is there are lots and lots of digital needs out there not being filled. People are more than happy to hand over their money, as long as you give them a great product they want or need. The Cyber Ocean Strategy says — deliver it digitally.

An example: my son is a competitive gymnast and I go to all kinds of gymnastics competitions now. The first competition I attended, they announced all the scoring would be done on a platform that had an app, and we could track all of the scores and rankings as they happened in the competition. This was, and is, absolutely brilliant. It's impossible to track the standings on your own and, of course, that is what all the parents wanted. When you looked around, every parent had the app live on their phones and tablets—a software developer's dream.

Think about that. Before this app there were thousands of parents who wanted this product, but there was no product. Maybe they didn't even know they wanted something like this until it was available. Now, because the judges use scoring software connected to an app, there is a need, a market — and an opportunity. It doesn't hurt the app can also be used for marathons, swimming, skating, skiing, and a bunch of other sports as well. The Blue Ocean Strategy guys would love this because the software company, instead of competing against everyone and their brother for CRM or ERP systems, cornered the market for recreational and competitive sports.

The key to digitally transforming is figuring out what needs to be digitally transformed. Look at that sentence again. Sometimes, the answer to all of your company's issues is to ask "what" before you ask "how".

Don't ask what the customer base you *have* wants. Ask what the customer base you have and *don't have* wants, and *what they can't get*.

One of the companies I worked with discovered their answer by my asking them one simple question, "What customers wouldn't buy from your company, and why?" The company had niched so completely that there was a set of easy to grab customers they had been excluding. After we figured that out, we found what we *could* offer them, and in fact, that we could offer it *digitally*. That one strategic question helped that company transform.

We can talk about Digital Transformation as a tool for renewal, but sometimes using a little Cyber Ocean Strategy can help a company mature and move beyond their core products and services.

Starbucks took this idea into a whole new business. First they made a natural evolution in their business because they thought people coming in for coffee might be hungry for more than sugar-laden treats. They started selling food, and expanded on that. But do you know what business their core products led to? The money-management business. Starbucks used that bricks-and-mortar base to load up $3.7 billion onto loyalty cards in fiscal 2013 and they expect that to blow past $4 billion for 2014. Starbucks mobile payment app makes that easier to buy, and even easier to pay. Starbucks is digitally transforming, evolving the right way, and reaping the dollars from it. They have the money for it, too, because who knows the percentage of loyalty cards that actually are used? They are in the money- management business and one thing — they know how to invest the $3.7 billion. In fact, their money managers were able to generate an 8% return for a cool $146 million in a 12-month period. That's a pretty serious evolution for a business that started off with some coffee beans and cups. A great example of deriving more dollars digitally from the customers they already have—from their core business!

Start looking at the world as it actually is — consumers spend a finite amount of money, and you need to do everything you can to get the largest share of it. Stop being scared about straying from your analog strategy because you are not straying, you are evolving. Let *that* lead you to your Digital Transformation.

Sometimes your Digital Transformation isn't obvious by looking at your own business. Sometimes, you find it by looking at somebody else's, and catching a digital piggyback ride.

Integration between different businesses continues to evolve; the model is not new. What is new is that it has become so easy. Think about it. Carpet companies are now flooring companies; grocery stores are now superstores with pharmacies, clothing and seasonal products, and Amazon, Walmart, and Costco sell almost everything now.

Starbucks is a good model for what can be found internally, but sometimes the answer isn't within your business. Sometimes it's waiting for you in someone else's business. Case in point: Pizza Hut joined forces with Xbox. Who would have thought you could combine video games with pizza ... wait a second, doesn't that make perfect sense? Kids are slaves to anything with a screen, and a nice percentage of that time is spent playing video games, so shouldn't they be able to order a pizza while they are playing? When you think about it that way it makes transforming sense, and Pizza Hut and Microsoft got it. Within 4 months of launching the Pizza Hut App, Pizza Hut sold over $1 million of product through the app. That doesn't really move the meter, since they do about $11.2 billion in sales worldwide, but look at what they did — they created a new digital market for their branded product, and they did it by using a digital distributor.

Can someone tell me why I can't order a pizza from my cable TV provider? Oh, I remember — because they digitally evolve like they're walking backwards, and will probably bring that one to fruition 5-10 years from now, about the time everyone starts printing pizzas with home 3D Pizza Printers!

Pizza Hut and Microsoft are titans, and that deal was all about business development. Create more value out of the gaming console, and sales for Pizza Hut (with most likely a fee to Xbox). Some of you may not be good at business development, or even in a position to hire someone who is. If not, there are all kinds of ways to piggyback. Amazon and eBay let people sell on the web and you can do it without breaking a sweat. If you have a product that they will allow you to sell on their site, and you haven't done it yet, put the book down and get it together. That is easy. Do it.

The trick is to find something you can turn into a sales conversion process. As I discussed in the digital marketing section, the web is not about blasting anymore; it's about targeting. Targeting the right person and, if you are lucky, at the right time. That is the difference between having a Pizza Hut app on someone's phone, and having it on the Xbox. Apps are great and a perfect way to get your digital feet wet by piggybacking on mobile, PC, and gaming consoles. However, everyone wants you to download their app and, for something like Pizza Hut, unless you buy pizza weekly, it might not ever be downloaded or used. But on an Xbox piggyback ride, you have a crowd that is the perfect demographic to nerd out and have pizza delivered to the door so they don't ever leave the gaming console.

At this point, we should all invest in Jenny Craig because the obesity problem is about to go ballistic.

# 19
## DIGITAL STUPID

### THE LEADING CAUSE OF DEATH FOR ENTREPRENUERS

I talk to business owners all day, and I love examining their models and helping them find the Digital Transformation gems. If you haven't listened to my podcast Start Attack (www.startattack.com) that is what the show is all about, talking to entrepreneurs and finding out what made them successful. It's addicting for anyone in business because what you don't always hear about is the innovation, motivation, crap, stress, sleepless nights, lawyers, and fun happening behind the scenes on the winding road to success.

What's clear is, despite all the digital change that the internet has caused, one thing hasn't changed in the business world. Everyone is good at something. Lawyers know the law, accountants know accounting & tax, a guy who owns a furniture company knows about furniture. Entrepreneurs on the other hand need to know about their own business, and then be knowledgeable about a bunch of other things they know nothing about and don't have time to learn. Every entrepreneur is born Digital Stupid. They only way to not be Digital Stupid is to put the time in. As a CEO, you might need to put in just enough time to understand how to hire digital smarts so your company is not Digital Stupid. I'm happy to say that many of the entrepreneurs I speak to realize they are Digital Stupid. However, this doesn't seem to be reflected in the masses. According to a report by Forrester Research called the 2014 State of Digital Report, 74% of

CEO's polled claim they actually have a digital strategy. Could that be true? Well, I know a lot of people that claim they have a great recipe for tomato sauce just like Nonna used to make, but most of it tastes like ketchup. I wonder how many of those digital strategies consist of a website, a Google Adwords account, and a Facebook page? Drilling down further into the report it reveals only 21% of CEO's of firms that have more than 250 employees set a clear vision for digital. Now that's a little more like what I experience, and is more in line with the Digital Stupid epidemic.

What really kills me about this report is it also states that in all but the biggest firms, CEO's are most likely to lay out the overall digital strategy for the business, but as the company size increases the CMO plays a significant role. OK. Now you just proved to me that you really are Digital Stupid. Again, this is not a CEO, CMO, IT, Finance, or Operations project—it's the responsibility and direction of the entire company and input and drive is needed from everyone. There is no way that all of these CEO's and CMO's are digital gurus.

So here is where it gets really interesting. Forrester also reports that only 15% of CEO's believe their company has the capabilities to execute the digital strategy. Now this I can believe because there really isn't adequate expertise out there right now to truly execute a digital strategy. I guess the 74% digital guru CEO's couldn't find the right resources, or pull that off by themselves?

The bad news is that Digital Stupid continues to be a full-blown epidemic and also an epidemic of denial. However, I am very encouraged as I continually meet CEO's who are not in denial and realize they are Digital Stupid. Here are two conversations I had recently with different entrepreneurs. This is exactly what they said:

*First Entrepreneur with a small business that has been at it for 3 years without much success: "Dominic, at this point I think it's clear that we are doing things in an antiquated way. We don't have a digital strategy, our competitors are killing us on the web, and I am spending money for SEO and other services that don't seem to get us anywhere. If we don't digitally transform this business then the doors are going to close."*

That conversation was not uncommon, but it really made me upset because I think the business has a lot of potential. It just needs an overhaul.

*Second Entrepreneur with a 20-year-old manufacturing business: "Dominic, here's the thing. We know we have a great product but the problem is nobody knows about us. We've been in business for 20 years and I just don't know how to get the world to know about our product. I think digital is the right direction but we don't know where to start."*

What was great about this entrepreneur is he was at least conscious of what was going on.

Do either of these quotes hit home? It's important to know you are not alone, and more importantly, to be open and honest that you are not supposed to have all the digital answers. You may be the best entrepreneur and CEO in the world and know how to make big deals, create strategic alliances, streamline operations, etc. but you don't know how to look at your future business through a digital lens. That's OK. I'm not an accounting expert. Maybe I know a little bit about accounting, just like you know a little bit about ecommerce, apps, and digital marketing, but I'm not out advising on the tax advantages of leveraged buyouts. That's the equivalent of creating a digital strategy.

We live in a world where everyone sells niches and we need to realize that our expertise is also niched. Don't let Digital Stupid be your demise. Find an expert or better yet, depending on the size of your company, you may have some digital expertise lurking there. Most CEO's don't know where to look for it internally, so do what we talked about and make it a company goal, game, or a contest to find it. You can afford to be Digital Stupid, but your company can't.

# 20

# TRANSFORMATION IS ADDICTING

## TWEAK BUT DON'T TOUCH

A t this point you might be convinced that you are going to go for it. You are going to digitally transform your business and start smashing the hell out of your industry. It is not only going to change your business, but it's going to change you as well. You are going to see things differently. Once you go through a Digital Transformation and start to see the benefits, your mind will begin to shift. You'll start thinking — a lot — about transformation and, sometimes, it might turn you into a transformation addict. That's not necessarily bad, as you must continue to evolve. However, it takes time to allow the transformation to bear fruit before you can squeeze out all the benefits. You can't understand the full impact of the transformation until you have lived with it for a while. You have to be careful not to make too many changes too fast, because it will become hard to distinguish what was successful, and what wasn't.

Because technology moves so fast, we expect whatever we do digitally will have an immediate effect. This is not necessarily true as market forces and rules are still in place. After doing a lot of different digital projects I have noticed that, whenever you put something new up on the web, it takes about 3 months for it to get traction. This may seem ironic considering the web is an instant mechanism, but it's true. Think about your neighborhood, and imagine a new business opening. It might take up to 6 months for you to walk by enough times to feel comfortable enough to walk through the door.

Of course, digital is quicker than that, but it has similar characteristics. If you have good analytics on your site, you may see a predictable pattern of return visitors slowly increasing. (If you don't know what analytics are, those are the things that track the visitors to your site. Get them installed on your site. Right now.) That's because people came by, checked out your site, and now that they are more comfortable they are coming back for a second look. This is why it is critical to get hooks into your customers on the first visit to turn that second visit into a sale. You may have a few hooks on your site that are working brilliantly but they need extra time and return visits to get your Christmas effect/ Strawberry Model/Draw, Comfort, and Close working. However, if you start changing everything at once it can be counterproductive to that flow.

Google sometimes doesn't tweak at all. Sometimes they build and release about 80% of a product offering, and don't bother to come up with the additional 20% unless they see the product gain traction. This drives many Google disciples bonkers, but Google is smart enough to realize that releasing a good product that is 80% done is better than never releasing a product that is constantly being tweaked. A good thing to keep in mind to keep your digital OCD in check!

Lastly, I mentioned it before and I will say it again. When you make a digital move either internally or externally, you need to test. Test it and get it solid before you send it out. I want to be clear that tweaking based on data from testing is OK. That is something that you should do constantly. However, complete teardowns, once you have initiated your Digital Transformation, should not happen. Tweak, but don't be a transformation addict.

# 21

## BLOWING THINGS UP

### IT'S EXCITING, IT'S FUN, IT'S LOUD!

Everyone loves hearing how someone kicked the establishment's butt, and made good doing it. That is why Biography Channel is so popular, and why I host Start Attack, because it is so much fun hearing about the journey. What you come to find out after speaking to so many entrepreneurs is that starting a business is hard; trailblazing is even harder.

The first time you read about Lewis and Clark, the definition of trailblazers, you might have asked yourself, what the hell was wrong with these guys? They must have had mutant DNA to head out into the unknown, uncertain how long it would take, what they would find, and not sure if they were going to be killed by the wildlife or the natives. What were they thinking? That someone had to do it, so it might as well be them? Because they thought riches and fame would follow? Or they just had that kind of spirit inside of them? Who knows what it was but there is one thing that I do know for certain, that the entrepreneurial spirit is connected to the trailblazing spirit.

I bet Lewis & Clark looked like hell when they got back but what they accomplished was nothing short of a miracle. When you think about it, trailblazing in the business world isn't much different. When you're the first in your industry to digitally transform, it's trailblazing. There are going to be days of excitement, pain, elation, confusion, depression, scrapes, cuts, and bruises. Think about what happens when you digitally transform an industry and blow it up.

It's LOUD because you don't do a smash and grab of market share without setting off all the alarms.

Digital transformation when done right will turn an entire industry upside down. It will be like trailblazing with a bulldozer instead of a machine. It's not quiet and it's not subtle. Several things will happen once you light the wick on a big transformation, so make sure you are absolutely prepared for them:

1.  People are going to say you are crazy. Definitely. Plan on all of your competitors saying that what you are doing won't work, and that it's stupid, and it's crazy. Ignore them, because...

2.  All of those people in point #1 that said you were crazy? You guessed it ... at some point they are going to copy you. All the doubters that put you down are going to jump on the bandwagon to get whatever you have. I remember in the funeral business all the old funeral guys kept saying there was no way anyone would ever shop for a funeral on the internet. They said funerals were a traditional business and people wanted to come into a funeral home. These guys were in denial, and were they ever wrong! I was on national TV on CBC's Lang & O'Leary Exchange, and they had me go head-to-head with a representative from the traditional funeral industry. This guy had the nerve to say that what we were doing wasn't new and that they weren't expensive and that they had always offered low pricing. Of course, I was more than prepared and proceeded to explain exactly how he had misled an entire national television audience. He crumpled a bit like his cheap suit after that. That was fun! Well, once we started kicking the butts of all those old traditional funeral guys the strangest thing happened. All of the funeral homes started revamping their sites to try and glob onto a little bit of our Digital Transformation. Some of them looked incredibly similar to ours. Some of them directly copied ours. They were all converted by the anti-Christ, a.k.a. the trailblazer.

3.  Not all businesses are covered by a regulatory body but a lot are and anytime you trail blaze they are going to freak out because you are doing something new. Every regulatory body that can

be, will be up your can with a thousand-power microscope. We experienced some regulatory hassling in the funeral business. When we asked why, all they could say was they had the right to do so. After getting hassled they finally figured out that we were doing things better, cleaner, and more transparent than most of our competitors that were complaining about us. They finally left us alone and realized we were one of the good guys. Sometimes being the first is damn difficult.

Speaking of fighting regulators, a buddy of mine, named Billy Shawn, was one of the original pioneers of the online pharmacy business. Billy was inspired to do something about the ridiculous cost of prescription drugs in the US. The year was 2001 and the internet was still in its post-bubble infancy. Billy started The Canadian Drug Store, the world's first online pharmacy, and he absolutely smashed the marketplace. He fought off regulators in both the US and Canada and won! They finally changed the legislation to stop him but he had already made his mark. Billy went from a tiny start-up to a digitally transformed cash register.

Now, Billy is firing up another venture and it has all the makings of another master class in trailblazing. Billy was a guest on www.startattack.com on episode 3. Go give it a listen either there, or on iTunes, to hear his exciting story.

Trailblazing is worthwhile but it doesn't always work out. Do you remember when online grocery shopping first hit the scene? PeaPod is the first name that comes to mind but Webvan was the one that really made the headlines. Unfortunately they made headlines because they filed bankruptcy and were one of the biggest casualties of the dot-com bust. Every business has all kinds of problems but Webvan also had to contend with the fact that they were trailblazing and one of the first.

One of the first to:

1. Get people to understand how it works.
2. Get people to want to buy groceries online.
3. Get people to feel the process was safe and OK.
4. Get people to feel the company was OK.

You may count that as only four firsts, but man o' man they are big ones. Especially the fourth one because building credibility is the Holy Grail of the virtual world. However, the second one is also tough because buying pictures on a screen instead of touching and feeling groceries is a process of adapting and evolving. That concept of physical to virtual is what every trailblazer who has digitally transformed an industry needs to contend with. However, changing a ritual that people perform on a daily basis is one of the hardest. Now combine that with a physical product that can't be digitized, like food, and a daily ritual like grocery shopping, and you have one of the hardest combos to initially get your audience to convert.

So, it was exciting back in 1999 and 2000, to imagine how Webvan and Peapod's model would try to change centuries of feeding ourselves. I guarantee all of the competition told them they were crazy! Peapod fortunately had founders who truly understood the grocery end of the business, and also the front-line business as well, because they had a small family-owned grocery delivery business in Illinois. This gave them a solid foundation to build upon and digitally transform the industry.

Peapod is really one of the original trailblazers in this industry and of course had an advantage as first-to-market mover. They were the trailblazers that really blew up the model and proved that digitally transforming the grocery industry was possible. But there is a saying, "Sometimes the second entity to come to market is the one who really succeeds." Ask Yahoo or AOL about Google, or Myspace about Facebook. For that matter, ask Facebook about Instagram (probably why they bought them) and Pinterest! People copy trailblazers. It happens. Peapod is feeling the heat from companies like Fresh Direct and a bunch of other companies.

When the titans feel like crushing puny mortals you need to wonder how valuable your first-to-market advantage really is. Enter Amazon Fresh. Amazon has tested their Amazon Fresh in the Seattle area and has now decided to take over the market. Literally. The guys at Peapod who cleared all the hurdles have blazed a beautiful path for the likes of Amazon and whoever else would like to enter the market. Did Peapod get a huge advantage from being the first? Yes. Do they still have an advantage? Sure they do. Only time will tell if Amazon will make a dent in their market share, or if the gravitational pull of the Amazon black hole sucks up a significant amount of customers. This one will be interesting to watch.

Last but not least, let me give you my story.

When we transformed the funeral industry, it was still in the dark ages. It was 2009. The concept of not having an actual location was my business partner's idea. These days fewer and fewer people want to go through the traditional funeral home process, and location is less important. His original idea was to give people what they want for less money. A great start. The way he wanted to execute this was to buy a van and ask his funeral director friends at competing funeral homes to send him business.

I had a different idea that followed my "own your customers" motto. What if you could take the entire funeral process and put it on the web? What if people could arrange everything, build themselves a quote, and have the cremated remains of their loved ones delivered right to their front door? Not only was this a new concept for people, but it sent a shockwave throughout the funeral industry.

Oh! They hated us, and they did everything they could to try and stop us. You name it. They tried the political route by trying to get the regulatory bodies to pronounce what we were doing was illegal. That didn't work because the regulatory bodies weren't going to play ball with them.

Then they tried slandering us by falsely telling people we weren't licensed and that our funeral directors weren't licensed. More lawyers' letters, and of course more apologies from them. Then they convinced all the main casket companies not to sell to us. No problem, we got nicer ones from somewhere else. Then they tried to get a lot of the tradespeople in the industry to not serve us, and we crafted another work-around.

So, not only were we dealing with all of the normal things that happen in a Digital Transformation, but we were also fighting a ton of dirty tricks courtesy of the oldest old-boys club around. However, we persevered and fought and problem-solved, and in the process showed everyone that we were the good guys by doing all the things you need to do to make it through. There were a ton of other growing pains but my digital concept has stood the test of time, and that is true trailblazing.

Are there going to be a ton of competitors coming to the table after you transform? Sure, and they will probably have a much easier time. Knowing that, would I do it all over again? Absolutely, as it was fun, I learned a ton, and I learned a lot about myself. Which is why I love starting, incubating and helping companies succeed with Digital Transformation.

What's the moral? Don't be shy about shaking things up a bit, or rocking them to their core! Ask the questions. Is your market feeling mature and on its way to being old? Has everyone fallen into the same old, same old way of doing things? Do you see a need that isn't being filled for customers or, conversely, are you not flexing to how your customers want to do business with you? If any of these conditions exist — especially if all of them do — it's time to trail blaze a new path in your company and even your industry, and discover a massive pool of new business and new energy. When it comes to Digital Transformation, it's going to be LOUD, it may be painful, and if you execute it incorrectly, you might crash and burn. But you can almost guarantee that it is going to be one of the most exciting things you do in your life.

## 22

## TRY, FAIL, SUCCEED: IT'S A PROCESS

### GET UP!

It takes a lot of courage to go out there and blow everything up. To be a leader or an entrepreneur you have to have courage like a lion, but after being eaten alive a couple of times you may end up feeling more like a lamb. Now you're scared and hide behind past failures as an excuse for not trying anything new with your business. Poor leaders use excuses like, "Oh, we tried this and we tried that and it didn't do anything." They feel that allows them to turn off all innovation and coast with what they have. Wonder Theory is gone from their lives.

Now, all they do is play it safe, and whine how their business is not doing what it is supposed to do and can't generate more customers and revenue. They are so afraid of failing that they have stifled their entire business because they won't try anything new. Failing is part of succeeding and there are a ton of clever sayings from some very brilliant people about just that. Sometimes failing is caused by external forces, sometimes it is a result of trying new things, and sometimes it is because you didn't try new things. So, instead of a smart saying, I am going to give you a few short stories about getting my ass kicked — over and over and over again — and how I dealt with it.

Incidentally, any problems I have ever had look like high-class annoyances to anyone battling it out in the 3rd world. Keep things in perspective — we have no excuse not to persevere through our failures. Keep getting up because if you do, that's a recovery and not a failure—this philosophy is what has fueled my ongoing personal transformation into the guy that just won't stay down.

## DOWN AND OUT THE FIRST TIME

I was born in Chicago into a tumultuous Italian family. I was always a bit confused why my life didn't resemble TV shows like The Brady Bunch, Family Ties, Growing Pains, or The Cosby Show. Instead, living with my dad was more like a Scorsese movie with him playing a cross between Henry Hill (Ray Liotta) in Goodfellas and Jake LaMotta (Robert De Niro) in Raging Bull. When I was 13 my parents moved the family to San Diego. San Diego was amazing but it was a tough transition and at 13 it seemed even tougher. By the time I was 15 my mom finally worked up the courage to leave. I was so happy for my mom, but not so much for me. I was left at home with my dad and my brother, and about a week later my dad started living at his girlfriend's house (pretty good reason for my mom to leave in the first place) and I was left with my 17-year-old brother who was nothing short of a tyrant.

All my friends and I called him Chet after the mean older brother in that 80's classic, "Weird Science". Chet had his 80's rocker girlfriend over every night, and they would smoke pot, watch porn, and crank the music all night. There was no parent supervision, no food, no money, nothing. I was destitute in one of the nicest neighborhoods in San Diego.

It was time for a Pivot and Go! I had worked construction the previous summer, so I knew how to work. I picked myself up, got a job to feed myself, made sure I did all my school work, and even managed to be voted most valuable member of the wrestling team. (Lots of teenage angst to get out.)

*When failure is thrown at you, Pivot and Go. Sitting around lamenting is time wasted. Get up.*

## DOWN AND OUT THE SECOND TIME

Things started to turn around about eight months later when I was 16. I worked construction again in the summer. My mom got back on her feet, and found an apartment for her and me to live in. At 17 I decided I was done with high school and wanted to skip 12th grade and go straight to college. I took a test, passed, and enrolled in community college.

In hindsight it was probably the worst idea I ever had. I missed out on the best year of high school. Did I mention that my high school was three blocks away from the ocean? Stupid!

However, I knew that I wanted to get a business degree so I could start conquering the world. As well, I was hanging out with an older crowd, and even though I was friendly with most of the people in my school, there wasn't much for me there. So, I took a chance and went to college, unfortunately with little to no guidance. I made money during part of the school year promoting American bands in Tijuana. Absolutely crazy in a rough-and-tumble world but an experience I wouldn't trade for anything. I was always trying to push past my years and, as such, I met a girl who was three years older than me, and soon I was out of the house at 17.

Before you knew it, I had bought my ticket to failure. I dropped out of second semester, and was quickly downgrading to first-class loser. I'll never forget my pathetic existence working in a golf club factory for just over minimum wage when I should have been in school. Then, my brother got me a job in a boiler room collecting bad checks where I learned the fine art of coercion. It was literally a 10x12 foot room with no windows and five greasy, sweaty guys making phone calls to collect bounced checks written to places like Domino's Pizza. Coming out of that cave at the end of each day, the sun blinding me the moment I emerged, gave me a very good indication my life was becoming a very bad movie. However, I didn't go down without a fight.

*The reason you take chances is to get ahead. Sometimes you fall back farther than where you started. Screw it. The time is now to make up for lost ground. Get back up!*

## DOWN AND OUT THE THIRD TIME

Something inside of me screamed I was being buried alive. That thing was called My Life. I knew I had to pick myself up again as I was destined for something greater than being a check collector. I put a plan together to get myself back in school and set myself on a long-term path to extreme success. My dad in a strange turn of events said he would pay for any university that would accept me. I figured he felt guilty by this point and respected the fact his son wanted to get a university education. Actually, I don't think he thought I could pull it off. I focused on The University of Southern California (USC).

I went back to community college during the day, smiled and dialed for bad checks at night, got the grades, and I was accepted to USC. I was going to be an international business student at one of the top ten universities in the West. I watched the first part of my plan come together and felt like my life was just beginning. I knew I was going to be a huge success.

I went through my first semester at USC and thought I had died and gone to heaven. Incredible professors, incredible education, an incredible experience. I took advantage of every opportunity to present my business ideas to alumni and received a great response. Not to mention I was going to some of the coolest clubs in Hollywood with virtually no money.

It was Christmas break and I came home feeling on top of the world. My older brother "Chet" also came home from living with this wild girl in Arizona. He decided he wanted to get his life back on track and go to college. My divorced parents called a family meeting. Well, that didn't go over well because my dad was insensitive and didn't really care if any of us went to college, even though I was already going. He said no. I defended my brother. Yeah, I know it's crazy that I stood up for Chet like that considering he made my life hell for years but life is too short for grudges and I love the guy!

The old man was severely pissed off and stomped out. Four days before second semester I called him to see when I could pick up my tuition check before I went back to school. His exact words were, "I'm not paying for you to go to school." After a lot of back and forth I was exasperated and that was pretty much it. Four days before second semester, no tuition money. And four days wasn't enough time to secure government financial aid or even a student loan. I went back to school, got all my stuff, came back home, found an apartment, and got a job as a waiter. The successful life I planned for was over. I was 19.

I tried going back to community college, but after USC, community college felt like a joke. One day I looked at a long line of people at the administrative building, looked at the parking lot and said to myself, "I'm done. I'm going to be a musician." By the time I got any traction on the musician dream, I was almost 24.

*You take time to plan everything perfectly but life throws a bag of anvils on your head. Sometimes disaster presents another path. Don't lament, invent. Transform, Get up, Go!*

## DOWN AND OUT THE FOURTH TIME

I played music for almost 10 years. After playing professionally, touring, travelling, and promoting, I finally had enough. The last straw was a grueling 23-city tour in 28 days with 7 guys in a van. It's funny how it started feeling like the check-collecting boiler room but with an even worse odor.

I knew it was time to get back to my business roots but I wasn't sure how to get there. I had been a musician for the past 10 years and needless to say I didn't have a resume that screamed experience. To make things worse, I was an American living in Toronto, Canada as a visitor with a very slim possibility of getting a work visa. I remember sitting in my apartment with no work visa, no job, very little money, little work experience, no resume, no clue, and honestly feeling pretty depressed. I was 29.

*You chose a path, you committed to it for the long term and it didn't work out. I guarantee you learned something from the experience! Now you need to get right back up and try something else. Like, right now!*

*"There ain't no power around, that can keep a good man down."*
*-- Sammy Hagar, Van Halen, "Get Up"*

## DOWN AND OUT THE FIFTH TIME

Well, if being down and out four times before had taught me anything, it sure taught me you have to get back up again — and more importantly, how to get up again.

I got my resume together, and talked up my marketing experience promoting shows across the US. After reviewing my resume, I realized I had a little experience. I was engaged by this time and my fiancée (now my wife) lived in Toronto, so I figured sweet home Chicago would be a quick plane ride away and a good city to find a job. Not to mention I had some family there.

I sent out my resume. Of course, nobody responded to it. So, I picked up the phone and started cold calling sales managers in the telecom industry. Once I had them on the phone, I was almost like the Wolf of Wall Street with my take-charge attitude, and told them that they had to hire me as I was going to be an incredible asset to their team. I verbally bludgeoned them into submission and had four job interviews booked and that ended with four offers.

I went to work for WorldCom and, after being misplaced, I walked into the sales manager's office I wanted to work for and told him he had to hire me. He was impressed by my energy and hired me on the spot. I was told to train for two months and not to cold call anyone for at least the first month until I was fully trained. I didn't have time for that and I was like a rabid dog that just hammered the phones like crazy. I guess working the phones in the check-collecting boiler room came in handy because I exceeded my two-month quota in the first two weeks.

Things were going great at WorldCom, and then things started to fall apart as the company imploded in one of the worst accounting scandals of all time. They stopped paying our commissions, and it got ugly. Acting on nothing but a hunch about a potential position, I looked at my wife and said, "Pack everything, we're moving to Canada. I'm going to show up and not let them say no." We packed and I crossed the border as a visitor.

I remember it was March 1st when we arrived, and it was a Saturday evening. The next day during Sunday dinner my father-in-law looked at me and said, "You're not going to get a work permit for a long time. Come to work construction with me." That just scared the hell out of me because I was not handy and I had put in two years of construction at 15 and 16, and I knew I hated it.

I lay in bed that night, thinking to myself, "I am in my in-law's house, no job, no work permit, and no certainty about the future." The one thing I did have was hope. The next morning I warmed up all my contacts, and within hours I had an interview lined up at Bell at 8:00 a.m. the next day. I showed up at 8:00 and by 8:30 they offered me the job I came to Canada for in the first place. My boss (who still is one of the greatest bosses I have ever worked for) said he would help me work through the red tape to get a work permit. A month later I was working, and went on to do very well.

147

*There are no rewards without taking chances. Calculate, mitigate risk, and weigh the options but at some point you need to leap. Keep leaping until you make it to the other side.*

The rest of the story is for another time, another book and though there have been rocky times since, I have been fortunate enough to have experienced a lot of success. I have had a life of incredible opportunities, and have built up an almost bottomless reservoir of energy and determination because I have made a career out of taking the leap.

Taking leaps means you are going to fall sometimes and even miss the ledge completely. That's OK. If there is one thing I can tell you about being an entrepreneur or business leader it's you have one unspoken job: Get back up after being knocked down.

In fact, that *is* the job because the knockdowns are endless. Big or small, traumatic or benign, it doesn't matter because you need to get back up from every one of them. Remember, it's not a failure if you get back up, it's a recovery. Digital Transformation may be a leap, but you have to try, transform, evolve, kick ass, crush old ideas, be an absolute force of nature and, more than anything, be unstoppable and take the leap!

# 23

## YOU'RE READY FOR TRANSFORMATION

### I MEAN IT!

Now you know what Digital Transformation is, why you should do it, and even how to get started. You need to make the commitment, and stick to it. There isn't much more that I can say to you except, apprehension about making a big move because you're worried you'll make a big mistake is every CEO/ entrepreneur/ hired gun's fear. You can take some comfort in the fact that digital mistakes are much easier to fix than say, retooling a factory for more efficiency, or investing serious capital to expand into another country. If it doesn't work, you turn it off; if it only works 50%, you keep that 50 and figure out the other 50.

Digital Transformation is going to be the lifeblood of your future business. If you are part of a business succession then make this one of your key initiatives. You don't want to be part of the digital die-off that's coming because it will be like a 500-foot digital tidal wave and you better know how to surf.

You need to add Wonder Theory to your leadership skills and your company's culture. You need to use that Wonder Theory and come up with a Digital Transformation that is going to shake the world to its core with Revolution Delivery, innovative Digital Hooks, and bring it all together with Dynamic Interaction. You know enough now to either start working on the skills, or bringing in talent that already has them. Whether you embrace the magic of the Christmas Effect, or use the Strawberry Model to get your awesome offering into a Draw,

Comfort, and Close model, you will turn digital into sales. You must tune your mind to Digital Transformation and take the first step.

Whatever you do, don't be afraid to make a mistake, because mistakes are pieces of raw rock waiting to be hammered apart to find the gold inside. And don't let past mistakes hold you back. You need to say to yourself right now that you are not going to sit around and do nothing. If you try something and it doesn't work, you are going to try something else because that hiccup, failure, mistake, or whatever you want to call it, was just one further step towards success.

Let me leave you with this. Art Blakey is known as one of the greatest jazz drummers ever. He was well known for his tremendous passion and fire, and for bringing young raw talent into his band and transforming them into superstars. One of his records included an outtake of him stopping the band and giving them a piece of his mind after they made a mistake in a section of the song. The issue wasn't that they made a mistake, but instead, they chose not to play anything in that section because they were scared the mistake would be heard. They did nothing! So Art Blakey said in his gravelly voice, "Stop. If you are going to make a mistake, make it loud so you won't make it next time!"

Now that is good advice. The time for doing nothing has passed. Get up, Go get 'em and smash 'em!

# AKNOWLEDGEMENTS

How do you list so many people with so little room, when you feel like you are constantly learning from all of those around you?

**First and Foremost:** This book would not exist without my impossibly patient and loving wife Christine. Nothing in the world seems to be possible without you. Arisano, Mia and Fiorenzo your inspiration is an eternal source of energy. Daddy loves you.

**First and Longest:** Thanks to all of my oldest friends. Andreas for showing me how to take a chance, Rob for constantly educating me and Sammy for keeping me grounded. Mikey for being a great friend and business partner and Fooch for being Fooch. Georgie for being the real deal.

**First and Instrumental:** John Mueller for teaching me responsibility, Gilbert Castellanos for giving me a chance, Wix for being there, Jay Erazo and Michael Lange for giving me a shot, Jenny C for fighting for me, Ward Maxwell for being a wonderful editor and making me a better writer, Mike Booth for the confidence, and Ed Minich for being the mentor I always needed.

**First and Influential:** Richard Reid for our educational walks and talks, the CEO gang: the three Mikes, Aaron, Erin, Paul, and Doug, David and Michelle Lewis for seeing value. Sunset 6, Jeff & Paul and of course, Canary Sean and Danielle.

**First and Friends:** The Wolf Pack, My PC Crew, The Venters, Marie, Lori D, Dr. Peter and Zen Irv.

**First and Family:** Mom, for teaching me to believe in myself, Nonna and Poppy for raising me with love, Chet for pushing me, Mama, Ata, Petey, Christina and Lily for the stability, all the Zupancics and spouses for giving me roots, Facchinis for a 2nd family, Aunt Linda for being cool, Pete W, Uncle Vic for making me creative, Uncle John for making me funny, and Dad...I hope you're up there looking down with pride... at least I have nice shoes!

# ABOUT THE AUTHOR

Dominic Mazzone is a serial entrepreneur and digital guru with what one might call an accidental voice created from a life that has seen more curves than an excursion up a mountain. However, that is exactly what is has been from living in various cities and towns in Illinois, California, and Ontario, Canada and working and creating in several industries, disciplines, and positions. Dominic is the culmination of a life of paying dues and fighting in the trenches. He remains a serial entrepreneur and also utilizes his guruness(not a real word) to help incubate and consult business to massive growth and digital domination. Working to live and striving to spend every free moment with his family.

Learn more at www.dominicmazzone.com.

CPSIA information can be obtained at www.ICGtesting.com
Printed in the USA
LVOW07*0238050615

441315LV00004B/31/P

9 780993 957321